HOW TO BECOME
A BETTER
EXECUTIVE RECRUITER
...AND HAVE YOUR CLIENTS ADDICTED
TO YOUR SERVICES!

Michael J. Palumbo

The Palumbo Company
PO Box 1998
Fairhope, AL 36533
www.thepalumbocompany.com

Library of Congress Control Number: 2009900626

Published by LuLu.com
Manufactured in the United States of America
ISBN 978-0-557-04137-4

To my wife, Katja, for putting-up with the highs, and lows, of this crazy business called executive search and professional recruiting. For my sons, and future recruiters, Tony and Leo. To all of my family and friends, in the United States and Finland, thank you for all of your love and support.

CONTENTS

ACKNOWLEDGEMETS

Through the years there have been so many clients, candidates, colleagues, family members and life situations that have refined and influenced my thinking in the executive search and professional recruiting business, but there was one guy very influential in my career, and he has left his mark throughout this book, and that was a guy we used to call "The Little General" or "The Genius" The late great Michael Latas. Thank you Michael for everything you taught me, you were the greatest!

INTRODUCTION

This is not your ordinary executive search, professional recruiter, or employment agency book. This is a book designed to get the most out of your firm and how you can be the <u>best</u> executive search, professional recruiter, or employment agency.

Although a lot of what you read in this book will be coming from an executive search prospective, all of the practices will be transferable to any firms that deal with companies (clients) that are looking to hire the best possible talent (candidates) for any given position.

Throughout this book I will be using the terms "clients" and "companies" These two terms are interchangeable and can be best described as the employers whom are looking to fill positions. I will also be using terms like "candidates" "talent" and "top-talent" "top performers" These terms are also interchangeable and can be best described as the employee, or person getting the job.

This book is titled, *How To Become A Better Executive Recruiter…* so it assumes you are in the recruiting business in some capacity, either as a solo practitioner with your own firm, a member of an employment agency or executive search firm. If you are a corporate recruiter, some of the topics discussed will not be relative to your day-to-day activities.

If you are new and just starting in the business, some of the information in this book may be over your head, but as you get more experience and start building up your practice you can reference this book later for some helpful *hints*. If you are a seasoned veteran and you want to pick up some new ideas or if you are looking for ways to increase your billings, deal with clients and candidates more effectively and help retain clients and get more referrals, you might find a few helpful *hints*, as well.

I think we can all agree there are so many different methods to recruit and make placements with our clients. If what you are currently doing works for you, by all means, keep doing what you are doing. But if you are looking for a way to increase your repeat and referral business, and your staying power and longevity in any market, then this book is for you.

The ideas and strategies in this book are exactly what our firm deals with on a day-to-day basis. These are the things that have helped our firm grow through the years. To the point where 95% of our clients are repeat clients, and for that matter, almost impossible to lose! And, the other 5% are referrals from those clients!

How do we do it? What are the methods? What is the magic? Why do so many clients keep coming back time and time again for us to help them find top talent? I hope this book answers all of those questions and maybe you to can learn *How to Become A Better Executive Recruiter…and have your clients addicted to your services!*

PART ONE

THE BIG PICTURE

Chapter 1

IT'S NOT ABOUT YOU!

The first step to becoming a successful recruiter is you have to realize <u>it's not about you</u>! Wow! What a way to start a book about becoming a better executive recruiter, right? <u>It's not about you!</u> Provocative? No, but it is the first chapter for a reason.

It's only about you when you consider the amount of research, sourcing, recruiting, consulting, and "handholding" you do to fill your positions, but that's an internal thing, like inside baseball stuff. That's inside information we know about, but most of the time the client has absolutely no idea what is involved to fill positions. In the end, your firm will be judged on the quality of the candidates you place. Period. And, the quality of those candidates placed will directly reflect the amount of repeat and referral business you will receive.

When a company hires you it is because they have a need. Period. Typically, they do not care how you fill your positions they want their position filled! They have no idea about the research, sourcing and recruiting it takes to fill your positions. In some cases, they probably don't want to know, they just want you to fill the position, as soon as possible!

One thing you have to remember, it costs a lot of money for companies to have a need, or an important hole on their staff, especially if it was unexpected.

The typical steps clients take to fill positions goes something like this:

Step one: Whom do you know?

Step two: Advertise the position

Step three: Repeat step one and two…

Whom do you know? Means just that, companies will ask around to see if anyone knows of someone that can fill a particular position. They will ask around the office, friends in the business, etc., the reason why they do this is because they know the results they are going to get with any advertising campaign…not much!

Advertise the position, Companies will start an advertising campaign in newspapers, trade magazines, employment and job board web sites, and their own internal company web site. And then they cross their fingers and hope that someone qualified answers their advertisements!

Repeat step one and two, Companies will repeat this step forever and ever, until they finally breakdown and realize they have to go to an outside source to fill the position. That's when you come in.

Once a client has hired your firm and determined they need to go with an outside source, at this point, they have become somewhat desperate to fill the position, however because there is a substantial recruiting fee attached to your candidates, they will not, and should not, compromise.

Hint: The longer a company has been looking to fill a particular position, they will tend to compromise a little more than usual.

When you get involved in a search, it is a race to see who can fill the position first, you and your recruiting firm, or the client. Most clients do not want to pay substantial recruiting fees, if they don't have to. So you better move fast, especially with all of the resources clients have today.

Yes it is true certain clients may like you, your personality, the way you presented your services, and your fee structure, however if you do not produce candidates they will not care a bit. You must understand, according to clients <u>it's not about you</u>! It's about the candidates you bring to the interviews and place with your client, because that is who they are going to be working with for forty to fifty hours a week, <u>not you</u>!

<u>Hint</u>: Do not assume a company is working with you because they like you. As soon as you stop providing good candidates and being a good source, they will stop using you. Just keep in-mind, <u>it's not about you</u>!

In our business, it is very common for recruiters to get big egos about how much they are billing in a month, or year, so let me be very clear on this…clients are paying substantial recruiting fees because of the candidates they are hiring from you. Period. The candidates they are seeing from your firm are "head and shoulders" above anything they have seen from their "word of mouth" efforts, or their advertising campaign. If your colleague in the next office, or at a different recruiting firm, called them with the same type of candidates the clients would pay these substantial recruiting fees to them, <u>not you</u>!

Never think about the money (I'll get into this more later). I have seen professional recruiters add up exactly what the fee will be when they fill the position, even before they start recruiting for the position! You always have to keep the clients and the candidates best interests at heart. If you start thinking of the money and how much you can make every time you take a search, it will taint your thinking towards both. And, remember this is about *<u>your clients being addicted to your services</u>*, right?

A few years ago, after I have been working with a particular client for many years and placed many top and mid-level managers, this client was telling me a story about one of his employees and how great he was. Let's just call him "Tom". This client went on and on and on, and said to me "if you can find me someone like Tom, that would be great!" And I said to the client, "well I remember how hard it was to get Tom on your team and it's not going to be easy to find another guy like Tom". And, to my amazement, this client said to me "did I get Tom from you?" There went my ego! This client didn't even realize he hired this excellent candidate from me and specifically from my firm. Wow! It made me realize something that day. I wondered how many clients really do not remember the people they have hired from us? That's when I really realized it wasn't about me at all.

In another situation, I was discussing recruits and setting up interviews with a very good client. We started discussing places they can meet for a lunch or dinner near the client's office. In the process of that conversation my client started to give me directions to a meeting place and then he, for some reason, interjected "so, where is your office located Mike?" There went my ego, again! I told him where our office was located and then we moved on to something else, but there it was again. Here is a good client, which I have had a good relationship for many years and placed several people with his firm, and he did not know where I was located! It's not about you! Believe me, I have learned this lesson and you should learn it too ASAP!

Hint: As long as you produce quality candidates for your clients, you can do this business almost anywhere…wherever you can take your phone!

So why did my good clients have absolutely no idea about the people I placed with their firm, or even where my office was located? Well, it's easy if you think about it. Our clients have so many recruiters calling them and they hire from recruiters all the time. Although it is true they like dealing with our firm, they really don't care where we are located, they want us to produce "top performing" candidates and fill positions.

Most of our clients are too busy selling their products, or services, to be concerned with small details. Besides, the candidates we place with our clients become the people they are familiar with and deal with on a day-to-day basis, not us.

It still amazes me how some recruiters, or recruiting firms, think because they have a nice office or belong to certain organizations, that is what makes them a better recruiter or recruiting firm. Not true, believe me, <u>it's not about you</u>!

Chapter 2

IT'S ALL ABOUT THE CANDIDATES!

In the professional recruiting business, the products are the candidates. We know the clients want to hire, that is a given. There are some companies that play games out there, but usually they are calling you because they have a need, or could not fill a position.

Remember, you and your firm will be judged on the candidates you place, not your marketing materials, web site, golf game, personality, or family stature. All of those things may get you the search in the beginning, but in the end, <u>it's all about the candidates</u>!

Once again, the quality of the candidates you place will determine the amount of repeat and referral business you receive. If you are not getting referrals or clients calling you back, most likely it is the quality of the candidates you are placing. A good test of this fact is to spend a day calling your old clients (the ones you don't deal with anymore) and see if any of the candidates you placed are still there. You will be amazed at the results of this test!

How do you find the best candidates? Obviously, first they have to meet the basic criteria of the search assignment and job description given to you by the company. Secondly, they have to be "top talent" in their industry.

Remember, the company hired you to find the best, not necessarily the most motivated or the highest paid candidate but, the one that matches the criteria of the search assignment and who is the best possible candidate willing to explore the opportunity.

Do not get hung-up on the motivations of the candidates; you need to find out if they are willing to go on a meeting. That is all.

Hint: I would rather have a company see the best candidates in a given market and not be able to secure them, than the client saying I did not send them good qualified candidates.

A candidate that is gainfully employed and competing with your client would qualify as one of the best possible candidates. I will go one step further, a candidate that is gainfully employed, competing with your client on a daily basis, and not looking, is even better. Not looking? Yes.

A candidate that is not looking and is currently employed, typically does not have their resume all over the country and speaking to one hundred different "headhunters" who are marketing them to three hundred different companies. This type of candidate typically doesn't have their profile, or resume on web site job boards. Most likely they don't even have an updated resume. I love to hear a potential candidate tell me they don't have an updated resume, because if they are not actively looking and they do not have an updated resume, you will not have competition with other recruiting firms and the candidate will automatically be a better candidate, just for the fact that they are working and competing with your client. This type of candidate will be "head and shoulders" above anything your client has seen through their advertising, or word of mouth.

I can hear you asking, again "How do I find this type of candidate?" I will get into this in more detail later in this book, but the absolute first and best way is to ask your client! What? That's right. Let your client know that this is a team effort and you are both in this together, trying to reach the same goal…find the best candidate for the position!

Ask your client for any names they would like to be added to the search assignment. Any individuals they may know in the marketplace that have good reputations and do good work. If you get some resistance from your client, get the names of the companies they would like this person to come from. If that doesn't work, ask them who they compete against in their industry, and which companies they admire in their industry. If that works, those are the companies to target first for candidates.

Hint: You will never know what you will get without asking. I have had clients send me lists, and lists, of people they want to meet!

If none of that works with your client, do some preliminary research and find fifteen to twenty companies in the local market that your client competes with and ask them about those companies one-by-one. This is a good technique because it shows your client you know the market, and it may also trigger some names from them once they start hearing the names of the companies. Sometimes when you first ask your client if they knew of anyone, you asked them cold and they really couldn't think of anyone, but once you start going through this list of companies they might start thinking of some names for you to consider in your search efforts.

Those are just some of the ways you can get your client to give you names of potential candidates for you to consider for the search assignment. It doesn't always work, especially if you are dealing with human resources, but it doesn't hurt to ask.

Secondly, and this requires a lot more work, is to take that list of fifteen to twenty companies your client competes with and find the best potential candidates within these companies and recruit them one-by-one until you find a candidate that matches the search criteria. You should not look for the most motivated, look for the best!

A good way to evaluate talent is to look at their track record. It is easy to tell how a potential candidate will perform in the future by looking at their past. How they have performed in the past is most likely how they will perform in the future. Thirdly, you want a candidate that is cooperative and does what you ask of them. Once you have determined you have a good candidate for the position and they meet all of the criteria of the search assignment, call you client and present the candidate and set-up an interview.

If you are doing this right, when you present your candidate to your client you will probably get a reaction from them, and you might even hear something similar to this "why are they looking?" "I didn't know they were looking?" and, of course, they are <u>not</u> looking you recruited them specifically for your client. Some clients (especially a first time client) will not believe it when all of your candidates are local and <u>not</u> looking, and hopefully you have a couple of local "Superstars" in there for good measure.

The reason your client will not believe this is because so few recruiters, or recruiting firms actually <u>directly</u> recruit! This is one of the big ways you can set yourself apart from your competition. Most recruiters do what their clients do, put "blind" post office box advertisements on web sites and newspapers and they ask around for "whom do you know?"

<u>Hint</u>: If you place blind advertisements in newspapers and job boards, you will get the same results as your client, before they hired you!

How do I know this is true? I'll give you an example of a true story that happened to me a few years ago.

I have a very good client in New York City and he belongs to the New York Athletic Club. Well, one day he was at the NYAC and a guy, somewhat of a friend, approached him about doing some recruiting for his company. My client had no idea this guy was in the recruiting business, so he listened to what he had to say. This guy was very convincing to my client, so my client decided to give this guy and his recruiting firm a chance. Besides, he was a member of the NYAC, he owned a New York recruiting firm, and my client's company is local, so why not? Since I have such a good relationship with my client, he called me and told me the story about using this guy he met at the NYAC and the reasons why he was going to use him. My client told me he really just wanted to "throw him a bone" and see how he performs.

After a few months, my client calls me and tells me how things are going with this New York City recruiting firm. I don't remember the exact quote, but it was something like this "I don't understand it, this guy's recruiting firm is based in New York City and he hasn't presented one candidate to me from New York State, let alone New York City!" "You're not based in New York City and every candidate you have every sent to me lives and works in New York!" "How is this possible?" After getting a little bit of the details from my client, like the first candidate this New York City firm presented to him was from Chicago, I knew right away this guy's firm wasn't <u>directly</u> recruiting at all. This guy's firm is the typical lazy recruiting firm out there putting advertisements on job boards and presenting my client with the first candidate who seemed to fit the search assignment.

Once I explained to my client the reasons why this guy's recruiting firm was doing the things they were doing, I told my client we were located in Alabama (he didn't know) and we have been working together ever since!

One of the things I've learned through the years, either as a recruiter, or training recruiters is we are lazy creatures. We tend to look for the easy way out. I have heard recruiters say stuff like "this candidate changes jobs every three years and he is on his third year with his current employer…he is due for a change". Of course what this recruiter doesn't think about is what happens after this candidate has only been with his client for three years! Oops.

Hint: What makes gainfully employed candidates so good is, they actually have more to lose than your client. They are the ones leaving a good position to join your client, so because of this, they have to make it work!

Your goal should be to place "top performers" with your clients. The reasons why are to numerous to mention, but "top performers" will typically stay longer with your clients and when they get on-board they will make a sudden impact and a huge difference in your clients operations.

Again, you will eventually be judged by the quality of the candidates you place with your clients. I know it's not easy to research, source and recruit the best possible candidates for your clients, but that is exactly how you will get more repeat and referral business.

Place the best!

Chapter 3

IT'S ALL ABOUT THE CLIENTS!

In the professional recruiting business, the clients are the ones that give us the searches, makes the offers, and pay substantial recruiting fees for our services. Basically, they keep us in business. The candidates are the products and the clients are the ones that hire us to find those products. And conversely, the clients are the products for the candidates. Obviously, you can't have one without the other.

It goes without saying you need to be recruiting for the best possible clients in any given market, or industry. The great clients are the ones that are simply a joy to recruit for. They do what they say they are going to do, they have low turnover, they pay market price or above for candidates and, most importantly, people want to work there!

It's all about the clients! You absolutely have to have excellent clients to recruit for if you want to place excellent candidates. It's that simple. "Top performers" want to work for top-flight companies, not has been, old run down firms in the community. Regardless of the money or position!

If you have ever had those "great positions" to recruit for, only to find out you cannot get anyone to go to work for that company, then you know what I am talking about. Sometimes it doesn't make sense, right? Well, wrong! Usually, it's the clients!

How do you determine the best clients? There are so many ways to determine which companies you want to target and which ones you don't. As a matter of fact you could write a whole book on that subject. Not to mention that companies fall in-and-out of this category, at any given time, due to management changes or changes in technology, etc.

So let's start by recognizing some of the obvious things to look for when identifying an excellent company to target as a future client. Bigger is not always better when evaluating potential clients. Instead of size, you should focus on the way that potential client does things or, the overall philosophies of the company. What kind of reputation do they have? How do they treat their people? Is there room to grow? Do they reward their people for producing? Do they pay market price, and above, for their people? Do they have a lot of turnover? Do they pay their bills? Are they a growing company? What type of growth? How many locations do they have?

Hint: Always look for clients with multiple locations. If the client has more than one location you will automatically have that many clients.

It is amazing to me, every time I have a candidate turn down a position it is always for the most basic things. It's the little things that seem to cause these searches to fall apart, isn't it? The client's general overall philosophies are the fabric of the company. How they go about doing things, how they act in a community, how they treat their employees, and how they treat other companies they do business with.

Remember, in our business the customers are <u>not</u> always right! In fact, most likely they need you and are hiring you for your advice.

It is important that they do what you ask, because most clients do not know how to attract gainfully employed "top talent" to their company. Most clients are used to hiring candidates that are out looking for a change and approached them. Is there a difference? Huge!

The ideal situation to be in with any client is when they need you, more than you need them. When you are dealing with a human resource department most likely they are on the "hot seat" because they can't fill a position through traditional means. These are some of the things to look for when targeting a potential client, and it can be a medium, or even small company that fits this description.

Once you have narrowed your list of targeted companies, based on the basic ideals and philosophies, now you have to get very specific. The research you did to get to this point doesn't get you the search assignment, right? You still have to call the company and get the search assignment. It may take you a couple of times to call and build up the relationship with this company before you finally get the first shot at a search assignment.

Hint: When you are recruiting in a market and you cannot get anyone out of a company, or it's seems nobody leaves that company, that's an excellent client to have. That's the one company you want to target as a client!

If you are a seasoned researcher, recruiter or consultant you probably have your own way of getting search assignments. But, if not, the best way is to call the highest position in the company first, and then work your way down.

So, if one of your targeted companies has a chairman of the board, call them first and work your way down to the chief executive officer, president and so forth. If it is a smaller company you will probably have to start with the president, or vice president, and then work your way down.

This next comment may get me in trouble, in some circles. Avoid dealing with the human resource department at all costs. If you have to deal with them, request to speak to the hiring managers for the positions. If you do not get them to agree to put you in communication with the person that will be hiring your candidates, you will regret it. You can always keep the human resource department in the loop, but you have to deal directly with the hiring managers to have any success.

For those of you that may not understand this, I will explain. Human resource departments are good for a lot of things but understanding how to attract gainfully employed candidates that are <u>not</u> looking, isn't one of them.

To be fair, there are different levels of knowledge and expertise within human resource departments and some of them can be very helpful. I caution you though, handle these situations on a case-by-case basis. You will find some of these human resource individuals can help you, and some may view you as a threat. You need to determine which side of the spectrum they are on before you start doing any recruiting for their company. Believe me, you do not want to go into a situation where the human resource department is sabotaging you, and your candidates, every step of the way.

Sometimes it's hard to determine which side of the spectrum they are on until you actually start recruiting for their company, but the sooner you find out the better. Once again, you shouldn't have a problem working or keeping the human resource department in the loop on every search that you do for a company, you just have to make sure to set the ground rules up-front before you get started.

<u>Hint</u>: If you want to start getting higher-level executive search assignments, you need to start calling on individuals at the higher levels, not human resources!

Some of these human resource departments, typically with bigger companies, have huge recruiting departments. You will find these situations to be better, as far as the recruiters in these departments have a pretty good handle on how to deal with gainfully employed candidates. You will still have to set the ground rules up-front before you get started, but generally companies with this type of set-up seem to be more in-tune with how professional recruiting firms operate.

When you get a search assignment from an excellent client and all of the candidates that interview with this client want to go to work there, your job will become so much easier. As I like to say, it's never easy, but at least when you are searching for that excellent gainfully employed candidate, you will know that you have an excellent client that knows how to merchandise the opportunity to join their company. Then, at last, you will really know that <u>it's all about the clients!</u>

Chapter 4

TELL THE TRUTH!

Honesty is the best policy in life, and it is also the best policy in recruiting. This is the easiest step, however it poses the most problems for some recruiters. They want to fudge the truth a little here and a little there, because they don't want to lose a substantial recruiting fee. Do not hike the fee by lying about the candidate's salary! And, never exaggerate the candidates experience, background and education.

In some cases, it might make you money and a substantial recruiting fee today, but you will lose a client down the road. It is a lot easier to keep a good client happy then it is to try and find another client. Any information you are hiding about these candidates will eventually surface and the client will find out, so why risk it? And, at that point, you will have lost a client and most importantly your reputation.

It simply is not worth it.

Hint: It's better to tell the truth now, rather than your client finding out later after they paid you.

I had a situation many years ago while placing a potential candidate, with a fairly new client at the time. When we were performing background checks on this candidate we found out he had a DUI in his past. Although it was a potential deal breaker, because this candidate was required to drive in a company vehicle in his position with my client, we decided to tell our client before they made an offer to him. Don't get me wrong, sometimes we hear things during the recruiting process that are really no business of our clients, and we leave them out. For example, a past divorce, a personal family issue, etc. However, a DUI when the candidate is required to drive in the new position is something you need to tell your client. Some recruiters would decide not to mention this to their client, for fear of losing a substantial recruiting fee. What happens when your client finds out? Are they going to ask if you did a background check on this candidate? They may say "didn't you know this position requires a lot of travel and we provide a company vehicle with this position?" How is your client going to feel about you and your firm? Are they going to think you are working on behalf of the candidate and not them? My point is, we do not know what they may be thinking, so we want to avoid this on the front end. <u>Tell the truth</u>!

In this scenario, I decided to tell my client the candidate had a DUI in his past. This was before they made him the offer. I figured it would be better if they found out up-front, before they made him an offer, but I gave them the chance to back out. You know what the client did? They thanked me. They thanked me for letting them know up-front, so then they could handle him differently during the hiring process. The client made the offer and ten years later we still have a good relationship.

Gaining the trust of your client is so important in this business, especially when you can provide insights to potential employees, what they are looking for in their careers and what kind of salary they are looking for.

It makes you on their team. Being one of the members of the team trying to reach the same goal, finding the best possible candidate for the position. You have to be viewed as an important piece of the puzzle. Someone they can count on to evaluate talent, give an honest assessment and tell the truth about your findings.

Don't hold back information because you think it will kill the placement. The exact opposite will happen, and you will have a client for life. The recruiters that hide information, or lie about candidates to make a quick buck, never last long. And they never have any repeat clients, or referrals.

It seems so obvious and simple doesn't it? Even if tempted, do not fudge on information, or keep information from your client. It is always better to tell the truth!

Hint: *Your reputation is all you have in the recruiting business. If you lose that, you will eventually be out-of-business.*

As professional recruiters we have dual obligations. One to our clients and one to any candidates we have interviewing, or in the process of discussing a potential opportunity. Just like your obligation to tell the truth to your clients, it is just as important to tell the truth to your candidates. Do not keep information you may know about your client from your candidates. Do not worry if they back out and do not want to proceed based on the information you told them about your client, you can always put the candidates in your data bank and use them later down the road. Remember your reputation is just as important to potential candidates as it is clients.

If you remember to treat the candidates and clients with respect, and tell the truth at all times, you will eventually have your clients, and candidates, addicted to your services!

Chapter 5

WIN, WIN, WIN!

A ny placement has to be a win for the client, win for the candidate, and of course, a win for you. If it is not all three, do not go through with the placement.

If you know something about the client and you are not telling the candidate, it is not going to be a winning situation for that candidate and their career. If you know something about the candidate and you are not telling the client, it is not going to be a winning situation for your client and their company. Ultimately, it will never be a winning situation for you if it is not a winning situation for the client or candidate.

When it does become a "Win, Win, Win!" situation it has an excellent feeling about it. It means you were hired by a company to fill a key position and you found an excellent candidate. Basically, you did exactly what you were supposed to do. This client will remember you and the next time they have a need they will use your firm. The client will remember your honesty and the way you handled the search process.

The candidate will remember how you were honest with them and when they have needs they will always be inclined to use your firm, and what is truly gratifying is they will always remember the fact that you helped them leverage their career.

To illustrate this point, I want to share a story with you about a very good client of ours. This particular client is in the construction business and the types of projects they build are these very large public works projects. Well, when you are building these types of government projects there are a lot of regulations to deal with. As a matter of fact, if you do not follow certain rules and regulations on these jobs, the government agency in charge can shut you down or, even worse, get you thrown off the project.

When we first received a phone call from this client he mentioned he was having some issues on a very large public works project, and if he did not get a new project executive to come in and take over this project, the government agency was going to throw him off the project. Not only was this going to be an embarrassment to him personally, it was going to be a public relations nightmare because this project was a very high profile construction project for a large metropolitan city. It was going to be national news story if the government agency stepped in.

Hint: The best search assignments are when your client desperately needs you. If you fill that position, you will have a client for life!

We took the search assignment, with a deadline of all things, and burned the midnight oil to find this client a new project executive to turn the project around. If we pulled it off, we were going to shine, if we didn't, there was a slight chance of us getting some of that negative press. Risky? Yes.

We pulled it off! We worked days, nights and weekends to make it happen. The hardest part, as you can imagine, was trying to find a candidate that had the risk taking abilities to come in and turn a project around.

We found an excellent candidate that was gainfully employed and <u>not</u> looking, but he was willing to take on a very large challenge and he knew it could make his career.

Was this situation a Win, Win, Win? Absolutely! The client kept the project, which turned out to be an award-winning project for his company that year. The candidate got his signature project, and he also won awards for turning the project around and saving the city money. And, our firm received a ton of repeat business from this client and we have had the most referrals from this client than any other client in our history.

Win, Win, Win! That one was truly awesome! All three parties, the client, the candidate, and the executive search firm won. If you stay focused on helping your clients win and stay focused on putting candidates in winning situations for their careers, it will be a lot more rewarding for you.

Chapter 6

DON'T THINK ABOUT THE MONEY!

One of the points I like to make to all new recruiters is "<u>don't think about the money</u>!" If your focus is on the money instead of finding the best possible candidate for your client, you will be doing this for all of the wrong reasons. If you do your job right, you will make money.

A common problem, especially for new recruiters, is working too light. If you are working a light caseload and hanging on every search assignment for a living, you cannot help but think about the money. Every search is do, or die! You NEED it, literally. If you could just close this next search assignment everything will be fine. The problem when you work light is, you need the money and it comes through when you are dealing with clients and candidates. They smell it. They can tell you are not looking after their best interests. If this is what you are doing, you need to pick-up your caseload and get more searches. It will make your life so much easier and it will make you a better recruiter!

Remember, this book is designed to help you get more repeat business and referrals. If you are trying to push a client to hire or push a candidate to take a job for the money, you will never have clients coming back for your services. If you want to stand out from all of the other recruiters, always look out for your clients, and candidates, best interests.

If you are always thinking about the money it will come across to the candidate and the client. Building up your caseload will help in this area, plus it gives you more flexibility in dealing with other clients.

Hint: Always focus on helping your client grow…as they grow, you will grow.

I had a situation a few years ago where a company called our office with a very critical need, and this company was a referral from another good client of ours so we wanted to help.

After explaining how we operate, this potential client said they heard good things about our firm, but they are not used to paying any money up-front for their recruiting needs. Now, normally in a situation like this, if the client is not willing to work under our usual fee structure, we will pass but, since they were a referral from one of our better clients, we decided to work with them. Besides, our caseload was heavy, so we could speculate on something like this.

We agreed to work with this company on a contingency basis, with the understanding that any future search work will be billed under our normal fee structure. They agreed.

The critical need position was a chief financial officer for this very good company located in a desirable area of the United States. It was also a confidential replacement. We took this assignment and burned the midnight oil to fill it. We filled the position with an excellent local candidate. We had all the risk. The client, under a contingency, had no risk.

We worked on this search assignment like they paid us a large retainer up-front. We were focused on finding the best possible candidate for the position, like we always do, even though it was a contingency search. The client never forgot this, and they have been a client ever since under our usual billing structure. Through the years we have placed a lot of individuals with this client, and they have provided us with referrals.

We could have never done this with a light caseload. When your caseload is built-up, you can speculate with clients under difference circumstances. When you are working a light caseload you cannot afford to speculate on situations like this, because you need the billings up-front to survive and stay in business.

Another thing, when I say, "Don't think about the money!" that doesn't mean lower your fee every time you are asked. No, the exact opposite, you should be very strong and stick by your fee arrangement. Once you enter into a fee agreement with a client put the money you could make, if you fill the position, out of your mind.

Hint: Once you set your fee and have an agreement with your client, never lower it!

If you are doing your job and providing "top talent" to your clients, the fee should never be an issue. I have had potential clients tell me they have firms they worked with that will do it for a lot less. I always tell them they should keep using them if they are satisfied with the results of the service they are receiving. Do not cheapen your service by lowering your fee.

Once again, the best way to keep your mind off the money is to build up your caseload. If you are doing your job, and staying focused on finding the best possible candidates for your clients, you will make money.

Chapter 7

ALWAYS PUT IT IN WRITING!

I f you are <u>not</u> documenting everything you do, you are making a big mistake and it will cost you money in the long run. You should always mark down the date of any phone calls to clients and candidates. Always confirm meetings with candidates and clients in writing via email, mail or fax.

Always have clients sign off on the fee structure before working on any search assignment, especially if you are working on a contingency basis. You should have some type of search authorization and spell out the fee clearly on these authorization forms. Back-up all discussions with paperwork.

I learned this the hard way. I had a situation with a new client and we were never clear on the fee. At the time, I needed a placement really badly so I covered this aspect of the search very lightly. Well, guess what? I placed a candidate and never got paid for it. I had a case to be made because I set-up all of the interviews, and helped the client during the offer stage. I really believed that this client was an outstanding company and would "do the right thing", but I was wrong.

The next call I received was from their attorney stating that his client (supposedly my client) didn't have any kind of contractual agreement with our firm to pay a fee for the candidate. Even though technically we had a verbal agreement, we never had anything in writing before the client made the offer and the candidate accepted the position. So we lost this fight. At the time, our firm was somewhat smaller and we really didn't have the resources to pursue this any further, so it cost our firm a substantial recruiting fee.

Hint: Always get some type of agreement with your clients up-front, even if you "trust them". It will save you time and confusion down the road.

Even with some of our very good clients we still back-up everything we do with confirmations in writing. You should confirm phone discussions and meetings with your clients and candidates. Believe me, even a good client will respect your professionalism and organization. It also cuts down on candidates and clients forgetting about meetings or phone discussions. You should also pass along phone numbers as well, especially if the meeting is after hours or on the weekend.

On many occasions I have had something come-up with the client, or candidate, and they had to reschedule a meeting. In a situation like this, it is always a good idea to provide everyone with contact phone numbers. That is especially helpful if the candidate is driving two hours to meet with your client. I have also had situations where a client, or candidate, cannot find a particular meeting place and because they had contact phone numbers they were able to make contact and coordinate a meeting place. Always put everything in writing, it will save you time and money.

PART TWO

THE BORING - DETAILED STUFF

Chapter 8

THE PRESEARCH

Always do a pre-search with any potential clients, before you actually get into the search assignment. A pre-search is a set of questions designed to figure out how long your prospective client has been looking, how serious they are about filling the position and what methods they are currently using to fill the position.

<u>Do not</u> let the company run you off the phone with something like, "I'll send you a job description" or "The job description is on our web site". Let them know that will be fine, but "Why is the position open?" and then continue with your pre-search questions. You really need to get into the reasons why this position is open before you proceed, it will save you time and money.

I will always do a pre-search on new companies and existing clients. If a good client calls me and says they have a particular position they would like us to handle, I always ask "why is the position open?" and continue with my pre-search questions. Believe me, this works.

If you are not doing a pre-search before you take a search assignment, you need to start doing them, it will keep you from working on search assignments that will never, ever close.

This is a list of typical pre-search questions to ask. You might want to tailor some of these questions to your specific industry.

PRE-SEARCH QUESTIONS

Why is the position open? This is the most important question to ask and how they answer this question will determine if you proceed. It is important for you to know what has happened, if anything, to cause this opening. The most typical answers to this question are, *confidential replacement*, *quit*, *fired*, *retired* or *retiring*, *promotion*, *expansion* and *newly created*. How this company answers this first question of the pre-search will determine if you proceed to the second question. You will be surprised how many times we get calls to our office and we never get beyond this first question of the pre-search "why is the position open?" We will pass on search assignments before we even get to the second question of the pre-search!

Because this first question is so important, let's cover those typical answers separately.

> *Confidential replacement*: You definitely want to know why they want this person replaced. The reason you want to know this is because you do not want to repeat the process. In other words, you want to make sure when you are recruiting for this position that you don't find a person exactly like the one they are trying to replace. So, ask a lot of questions on confidential replacements. This is, by far, the best search assignment to get from any client. If it is truly a confidential replacement they cannot advertise for this position. Basically, they would be relying totally on you to fill this position. Obviously, since it is confidential you need to ask your client where they would like to meet the candidates and where they would like all of the correspondents to be sent (because now you put everything in writing, right?)

Quit: You need to ask your client why this person quit. It is important to understand what reasons they gave your client. What if the reasons are "because we are closing that office" or "he didn't like working on Saturdays and Sundays" are these things you need to know before you take this search? You bet! You also want to know if this person is gone, or are they "quitting". I have had situations where I took the search, started working on it, and then the person decided not to quit. You want to avoid wasting time on searching for a position because someone "might" quit, or is "quitting". You need to make sure this person has quit, or is definitely quitting. If they are quitting, you need to know the date of their last day. Another thing you need to know is how long this person worked for your client. If this person worked there a long time it might be difficult to fill this position because this person will most likely be hard to replace.

Fired: Once again, you need to ask your client why this person was fired. Sometimes (especially if you are dealing with human resources) they do not want to tell you the reason. Let your client know that it is very important for you to know the reason why, because you do not want to find someone with the same traits as the person they fired. Really dig into the reasons why they fired this person the best you can. It will save you time and money in the long run.

Retired or retiring: You need to distinguish the difference between retired, or retiring. Once again, you want to know if this person is gone, or not. If not, you need to know the retirement date. You will want to know how long this person has been with this client, as well, because this could also be a search assignment that is very hard to fill because the person has been there so long. And, they may not retire after all. If the person is no longer with the company, that would be the best scenario.

Promotion: You need to get as much information about the person that received the promotion as possible, which is why this position is open. Are they going to be involved in the search? Will they be doing any of the interviewing? What did they like about this person? I personally like to hear promotion, because that means this company hires from within and that is one of the things you can merchandise when you are speaking to any potential candidates for this position. One of the red flags would be if this person whom received the promotion is heavily involved in the interviewing process, they might not like a lot of your "top talent" candidates for fear of a competitive threat. Or, they do not want someone in that position that would outshine them. Just something you should consider before agreeing to work on this search.

Expansion: Once again, expansion shows that the company is growing. This is something you can merchandise to potential candidates when you are recruiting for this company. You really do not have to do a lot of digging on this answer.

Newly created: Caution!!! This is, by far, the hardest search assignment to fill. Do not work on this type of search if you are new to the business, and certainly be extremely cautious about working on this assignment if you are a veteran recruiter. This search assignment will be a nightmare with a new client, or an existing client. They do not know what they want, because they have never had anyone in this position. My advice on this one is to pass. Let some other recruiter go broke on this one. Passing on this search will <u>make</u> you money!

How long have you been looking? If they just started or it has been shorter then a month that is fine. On the other hand, if it has been six months, or longer, you want to understand what type of problems they have been having. Sometimes it can be the position really wasn't priority for them, and now it is. If that's the case, you need to know what has made this priority. It is a good idea to get as detailed as possible before you waste your time.

How soon do you want this person on board? You really want to ask this question to see where this fits on their list of priorities. If they say in a year, or so, you need to pass on this search. This is considered a casual need. Let them know you are passing on this search, however if this becomes more critical for them, to call you. A lot of times when it is low priority for the client, they won't be as cooperative as a client that has a top priority need. It will take them longer to get back to you. They will drag their heels on an offer, etc. If it is low priority, pass on the search.

What methods or sources are you using to fill this position? You need to know if they have an advertising campaign, or if they have other recruiters working on this position. If they have a bunch of recruiters working on this position currently, I would pass on this search. It will be too crowded out their with all of these recruiters recruiting for the same position. The ideal situation is if they are only using you to fill this position. If they are running help wanted advertisements and you will be the only recruiter, that's fine.

How many candidates have you interviewed so far? You need to know how many candidates they have interviewed on this search, and if any of those candidates are still in contention, or if they have any offers pending. You will also want to know if they had any candidates turn down any offers for this position. If they have had a lot of candidates and a lot of turn downs, that's a red flag. You need to get as much of the details as you can before you proceed with this assignment. Obviously, zero is the answer you are looking for here.

Is this assignment tied to any future business? Some potential clients want to get ready for that big project they are "anticipating", but they really don't have the need right now. I would want to know what happens if they don't get this big project, or account. You need to know if they will still have a need and will they still hire a potential candidate, even if they do not get this project, or account.

Are there any in-house candidates in contention for this position? You need to find out if they have asked, or if they have someone in their company ready to step up and take this position. I have had situations where the clients said they didn't have any one in-house, but then cancelled the search and filled it with someone in-house because they really didn't ask around, or they didn't think that person would want the position.

If you do not get the answers to the pre-search questions to your satisfaction, do not move forward. The most important lesson to learn, especially for new recruiters, is which search assignments to work on, but more importantly, which search assignments to not work on. Understanding the difference will save you time and money.

Now that you have made the decision to move forward, based on the answers you received with the pre-search, the next step is the search assignment.

Chapter 9

THE SEARCH ASSIGNMENT

The search assignment is an additional way to get detailed information about the position, and it is used in conjunction with the job description. <u>Do not</u> use only job descriptions, they are very incomplete for what you need to know. You really need to dig into this position and all of the aspects of the job. The pre-search sets the stage for this step, which is the search assignment.

The search assignment is designed to go into greater detail then any job description or pre-search. As with the pre-search, when you are taking a search assignment you are really looking for additional problems with this company, or position, that are going to give you difficulties in filling the position.

Hopefully the company has a job description, if they do not, the search assignment will help you put together a job description for the company and for you. Obviously, if the company <u>does not</u> have a job description you will have to ask a lot of general questions that you typically see on job descriptions. As in, title of the position, duties and responsibilities, job requirements, location, etc.

Whether you have a job description, or not, it is very important to dig into specifics when trying to figure out if this is a great, good or poor search assignment this company is giving you. Digging will help you determine if you are going to pass or take-on this search. Do not work on searches you cannot fill. This is a big problem with new recruiters. You have to realize that if you cannot fill this search, there is no reason whatsoever to take it. It will only hurt your reputation in the industry and you will get a reputation that you cannot fill searches. Remember, we want to retain clients and get referrals. The only way to do that is to work on good searches and pass on the bad ones.

Now let's focus on the areas to dig into when taking a search assignment that are typically <u>not</u> on a job description. These are questions you should ask along with any job description provided by the company. You should put together some type of search assignment questionnaire to have in front of you when you are speaking to a potential client.

The areas of the search assignment questionnaire you should really dig into are, **duties and responsibilities**, **compensation**, **hiring procedure** and any **additional recruiting questions** regarding your efforts. Under these specific areas you should focus on a list of typical search assignment questions to ask. You might want to tailor some of these questions to your specific industry.

DUTIES AND RESPONSIBILITIES

Will there be any staff reporting to this person? The reason why you are asking this question is because you need to know how large of a staff, if any, and get the titles of the individuals that will be reporting to this person. Sometimes companies will give you a job description, and search assignment for a position titled, regional vice president or area manager and they will have no direct reports. You need to know this because if the new position has a big staff you will have to find a candidate that has big staff management experience. If you work on this search and start presenting candidates that have the title your client is looking for, but they do not have any direct reports, those candidates will not work. You are going to frustrate yourself unless you know the details of the staff, if any, so you know which way to go when you start recruiting for this position. If the position has a fantastic title but they do not have any direct reports, you may want to think twice before working on this search assignment, unless this is a standard practice in your specific industry.

Is there any overnight travel required? If they answer yes, you will have to find candidates that are open to travel. As you know, not everyone is open to travel and being gone from their family for any extended time. Heavy travel in a position is a situation where you will want to know how much travel, how long, where, etc. If the travel is extensive, you will have to use your best judgment if you can fill the position. For instance, if this position in your industry typically requires travel, then it shouldn't be a problem. I will only caution you on this, I have had situations where I took a traveling position and when I started recruiting, I found most of the candidates would only make a change if there was <u>less travel</u>, not the same or more. If they answer no to travel, that usually isn't a problem.

What are your thoughts about education? The reason why you are asking this question, even though education requirements are typically on job descriptions, is because you want to know if this company is open to interviewing candidates in their industry that are doing the same job now, but maybe they do not have a certain degree, or a degree at all. There is nothing more frustrating then to find an excellent local candidate that is in the same industry as your client, only to find out they will not bend on the college degree requirements. Most companies put degree requirements for positions as a screening tool, more so than a rejection factor. If this company is open to the educational requirements, that is fantastic. If they are not, you may want to pass on this search, unless it is for a specific position that most likely requires a license like a doctor, lawyer, engineer, or accountant. In that case, most likely when you start recruiting individuals in these positions, they will already have the type of degree your client is looking for, so it shouldn't be a problem.

What about years of experience? The reason why you are asking this question is because you want to expand the search beyond the number of years they have on the job description. Let's say on the job description the company has put five to ten years of experience required. You want to ask if they are open to see someone with three years of experience. Then you should ask if they are open to someone with fifteen, or twenty years of experience. If they are open to those years, you just expanded the search to three to twenty years of experience, instead of five to ten years, without the company even noticing it. Most companies will expand the years of experience with no problems whatsoever, if they don't, I would find out the reasoning for having the parameters so tight, and I would consider passing on this search assignment if they don't bend.

What is the potential for this position? The reason why you are asking this question is because most of the candidates you will be recruiting are gainfully employed and <u>not</u> looking, so they are totally looking for an opportunity to leverage their careers. They will be looking for the career path in any new position. If this company tells you "there isn't any" or "well, I never thought about that" that is a big red flag. You need to seriously consider working on a search if it doesn't have any potential. Unless there is an ownership situation, or a candidate has other motivations like where your client is located, it will be hard to fill any position with a company that offers absolutely no potential. Use extreme caution on this one. Obviously, you want to recruit for companies that have great potential and an excellent career path.

<u>Hint</u>: Clients always end up hiring the person they <u>LIKE</u> the best, over any other qualifications, or characteristics.

COMPENSATION

What is the salary range for this position? The reason why you are asking this question, and it somewhat ties into the years of experience, is for prescreening purposes. In other words, you do not want to waste your time with a candidate that is over the salary range. So, for example, if you ask this question and the company says something like "$85,000 to $125,000" you need to make sure the salary ranges they give you are in-line with the marketplace. A good thing to do at this point is to ask the question "if we find someone making $150,000 would you want to see them?" and if they do, you just expanded the search to $150,000. Another way to deal with a possible salary issue is to ask "do you have any flexibility on the $125,000 top base salary?" most companies will say they do for the right person. Now, you are not doing this just to get a higher placement fee, you are doing this to include as many candidates as possible on a search, and if you find someone that fits the search and is making close to the top of the salary range, you know they will have flexibility to attract them. Now this only covers the base salary, so you will have to get all of the details on any additional benefits. For example, bonuses, profit sharing, 401k, pension, vacation, company vehicle provided or allowance, medical plan, dental, vision, prescriptions, optical and any other fringe benefits. You will want to get the full details on the additional benefits, as far as, when they can get in these plans, how they work, how much they cover, etc. You will have to compare this company's benefits with any candidates you are dealing with for this position. If the benefits are out-of-line for the industry, or the market, you have to let your client know. I will not work on a search, if the compensation for the position is not in-line with the industry, or the market. Recruiting is difficult work and you do not need to make it more difficult with a company that has a terrible benefit package. If you cannot get them to change the benefits for the better, pass on the search assignment.

<u>Does your company have a relocation policy?</u> You need to know if this company has a relocation policy for the level of the position you are discussing. Some companies may have a relocation policy, just not for the position they are discussion with you. Make sure they have a relocation policy for the position, if you have to leave the market where this company is located. If you know you will have to leave the area and they do not have a relocation policy, I would pass on this assignment. If they do have a relocation policy get all of the details, including any interim living, house hunting trips, etc.

<u>Hint:</u> Relocations are the number one reasons why candidates turn down positions. If you can stay local during your recruiting efforts, it will enhance your chances of filling the search assignment.

HIRING PROCEDURE

<u>How many interviews and how long does it take?</u> The reason why you are asking this question is because most of the candidates will be asking <u>you</u> this question, so you need to know. And the other reason is because you need to know how long this company takes to hire. Do they want to speak by phone first? How many in-house meetings? How many people will be in these meetings? You need to make sure you have a clear understanding of how many meetings, what type of meetings and how long their hiring procedure takes. If the hiring procedure is extensive and requires a lot of people to make the decision, I would think twice about this search. It is hard to get one person to agree on a candidate, let a lone a whole group of people. I have had candidates get by the first way of interviews, the second way of interviews and the third way of interviews, only to get knocked out in the forth interview. No thanks. I advise you to get another search before you take on anything like that. So, what is reasonable? I would say depending on the level of the position, but typically three meetings and then an offer is sufficient. Anything else, I would look at on a case-by-case basis.

Is there anyone else who can interview? You need to know if someone else within the company can interview if your main contact, or hiring manager is out of town. This step will save you time. What if your main contact is on vacation for two weeks and your candidate is in town for only two days? It would be great if some else can interview your candidate, especially if your main contact cannot.

Are you free to interview nights and weekends? You need to know if they are willing to meet your candidates at night, or on the weekends, because most of your candidates will not be able to meet during normal working hours. I have had clients meet late at night, and meet on a Sunday morning. Do you think they want to fill the position? You bet. I have also had clients that would not meet after 5:00 PM or on the weekends, I am not saying they do not want to fill the position, but they sure are not being very cooperative.

Does your company do any testing? I cannot say this loudly enough. If they require any type of psychological testing for candidates PASS ON THIS SEARCH! If they have drug and alcohol testing, that's one thing, but if they have these crazy psychological tests that some companies do (and this comes in waves, year-to-year, depending of the part of the country you are in) absolutely pass on this search assignment. I do not have a problem doing testing regarding a certain skill that is needed for a job, or a pre-employment drug test, or criminal background test. There is nothing more frustrating than having an excellent candidate for your client that is well known in the industry, only to find out he cannot pass this crazy test your client makes them take. I have had this happen. Do not work on this type of search assignment unless the company agrees that your candidates do not have to take the test.

ADDITIONAL RECRUITING QUESTIONS

Are there any specific individuals or companies you would like this person to come from? You need to get as many names of individuals they want included in the search. Also, you need to know if they have any specific companies they want this person to come from. You will be surprised on the response you will get when you ask this question. Either your client will be total cooperative and give you names of people and companies where they want you to focus, or they will say "that's your job!" if they say that, you know you are not working with a very cooperative client. In this case you need to let them know you are in this together and you both want the best possible candidate for the position. You have to use your best judgment on this one. If they won't give you the companies, then I would pass. If they do not give you specific names of individuals, I would judge them on the total cooperation during the whole process. If they have been cooperative on everything else, it's not a deal breaker, but if they have been difficult during the whole pre-search and search assignment, I would pass.

Are there any "hands-off" companies? You need to know if some companies in their market, or industry, are "hands-off". The most frustrating thing, and it is really something that can demoralize a staff, is when you have the perfect candidate for the company only to find out because they have a relationship with the candidate's company you cannot recruit from that company. This can be avoided if you ask this question. Make sure you have all of the companies that are "hands-off" before you start sourcing and recruiting.

As you can notice by these search assignment questions most, if not all, of these questions are rarely answered in a job description. If you are not asking these questions now, include them from now on, it will definitely help you get a better handle on what your client wants, and most importantly, if you can help them!

If you cannot help them fill the position, based on the pre-search and search assignment questions, do not work on the search assignment. It will help your reputation greatly if decide to get more choosy on your searches.

Never accept, or pass, on a search assignment right away. Always ask the questions and digest the answers for a day, or two.

A better way to go about this is to tell your client you will review their company's information and their need with your staff and get back to them in a day, or two. If you want to call it a "staff meeting" or "staff allocation meeting" that's fine. But <u>do not</u> accept, or pass, right away.

If, after waiting a few days, you decide to pass on the search assignment go back to the client and tell them the precise reasons why you are passing. Sometimes, the client can fix the problems with the search assignment and make it a better search. For example, maybe you are going to pass because the salary is too low, or the title of the position isn't in-line with the salary. The client has the option at that point to raise the salary, or maybe change the title of the position.

I have changed searches from bad and unacceptable to very good and fill able. If you give your reasons why you are passing and let your client decide to change and fix the problems, or not. Let it be their problem, not yours. In any case, you will gain respect for passing on a search assignment if you give very precise reasons why you are passing.

If, after waiting a few days, you decide to take the search assignment you need to go back to your client and tell them you are accepting the search assignment and you need to give them a start date. Once again, I like to push this out a couple of days. Do not start right away you're busy, right? If it is a Monday, tell them you will get started on Wednesday or Thursday. Let them know that is when you will have the next available time to take on another assignment.

A major problem with new recruiters is working and recruiting on bad searches. If you incorporate some of these additional search assignment questions when a client gives you a job description, it will improve your chances of filling more positions, because you will be working on better positions and passing on the bad ones.

Now that you have all the right answers on the search assignment, and you have decided to move forward with this company and their search assignment, let's move on to the research and sourcing.

Chapter 10

RESEARCH / SOURCING

R esearch and sourcing is an art. Some of the best recruiters cannot do research or sourcing very well, so conversely they are not very good recruiters. If you cannot do research and sourcing, you need hire someone that can. If you are a solo practitioner there are firms that do this type of work, and they are usually ex-researchers and ex-recruiters that worked with larger recruiting firms. Typically, you can hire these firms on a per-project basis.

Research and souring is the most important part of the search assignment. If the research and sourcing are performed wrong on a search assignment the whole thing is going to be wrong. The research will have you in the wrong companies, and you will be sourcing the wrong candidates, within these companies. And, most importantly, your candidates will be wrong for the search. The candidates simply will not fit the position.

This step is not only one of the most important steps in the process it will also help set you apart from your competitors.

Most recruiters, or recruiting firms, do not <u>directly</u> recruit. They basically put together advertisements on web sites, job boards, newspapers and trade magazines, etc. Along with this step they will look for candidates on Monster, Craig's List, Career Builder, and industry specific trade associations, and societies etc. All I can say about doing things this way is, good luck!

You have to remember, your client is doing this as well, and has probably already done this before you got involved. All of these sources will be exhausted by the time you get involved in this search, especially if this is the way you do your research and sourcing. Any good corporate recruiter worth their salt will be able to do this, why do they need you? Plus, once you start sending over candidates, most likely they will already be aware of them. Is your client going to pay you a substantial recruiting fee for a candidate they are already aware of, or they have already interviewed? I don't think so.

So, what is the best way to do your research and sourcing? Here are some good ideas on how we have always done it. Of course, if what you are doing works, continue to do what you are doing, but if you are not getting the repeat business or the referrals you want, you might want to consider some of these ideas.

<u>RESEARCH:</u>

1) Include all of the companies and individuals your client gave you during your search assignment. Of courses, these are the ones you need to target first because this saves you a tremendous amount of time. Plus, these are the companies and individuals your client knows and likes! Why wouldn't you target these first.

2) Research a list of fifteen to twenty companies your client competes with. Remember to <u>exclude</u> the "hands-off" companies. Start in the local market and work your way out geographically. Do not go under a list of fifteen companies, if you have to go to another state, do so.

3) Once you have this list you need to figure out how many people within these companies do what your client is looking for. Some companies may have multiple individuals within their company that does what your client is looking for. For example, if it is a middle manager type of position they may have a lot of these

types of potential candidates for you to recruit. If it is a senior level executive there may only be one per company, so it makes it a little easier to source out the individual you need to recruit in that company. If it is a small company they might not have the type of person you are looking for. For example, in some small companies the president may be the owner, so if you are looking for a president this will not work.

Once you have the fifteen to twenty companies together, plus the ones your client recommended to you. It is important to make sure you have a clear understanding of the duties and responsibilities of the position. Review the search assignment and determine exactly what your client is looking for and what they hired you to find. A lot of times titles vary from company to company. In one company, the person you are looking for may be called a vice president of operations, but in another company that person may be called an operations manager. So, it is very important that you have a good handle on the duties and responsibilities, more so, than just the title of the position.

SOURCING:

1) Make sure you have the title of the position, duties and responsibilities and any additional information you may need once you start calling these fifteen to twenty companies. Make sure the individuals and companies your client wants you to target are priority.

2) Begin calling these companies and asking them who performs this function within their company for which you are searching. Start with the companies closest to your client and start moving out from there. You will be surprised what information you can get if you ask. Most of the time when you call a company for the name of their controller, or vice president of marketing etc., the person answering the phone will give it to you. If you start getting some resistance you may want to change your strategy and your approach.

This will take some time for you to master and for you to find out what works best for you. In some cases, you might want to use an alias to call into some companies, if they start screening you hard. Tell them as little information as possible to get the information you need. This is the private investigating part of the recruiting business. Remember, you have been hired to recruit a certain position for your clients. You need to find out whom within your client's competitors you need to recruit for your client. This is where you can find some directories that are specific to your industry and some information on the web, but you should be careful here, because a lot of the information on the web can be in wrong.

3) Once you have fifteen or more companies with names of the individuals within those companies, that hopefully do exactly what your client is looking for, now it is time to recruit these individuals! What I like to do here is prioritize the people within these companies I want to recruit first. I will put the companies that are the closest, and then, if there are more names in a particular company, I will prioritize which one I want to recruit first. Never recruit more than one person out of a company at a time. If the first candidate passes, then move on to the next person. If the first person you recruited is interested, do not recruit another one out of the same company. It is not a good idea to have more than one person out of a targeted company interviewing for the same position for your client. You are setting yourself, and your client up for potential angry call from a company saying "quit recruiting our employees!" Not a good idea, and it may hurt your reputation and your client's reputation in the marketplace.

Hint: Give as little information as you can to get the names. If you are uneasy about calling these companies for the names, you can use an alias. But, make sure the alias is made up and never use a real name of someone, or of a real company, or government agency.

Another good way is to ask people you know in the business, through your networking. Sometimes in our business people like to call this 3rd party recruiting.

A lot of times you can contact candidates you placed before, or recruits you know and have reached out to in the past. These types of individuals will typically have names to give you for what you are looking for. Some people will give names freely, others you will have to pull them out. For those, let them know you will leave their name out of it, if they give you any names. A lot of times people do not want to give you names because they don't want it to get back to them in a negative light, or they don't want to make a "recommendation". Let them know you will make the determination if the candidates qualified you are not looking for a "recommendation", just someone that can do the job.

Sometimes none of that seems to work either. Some people will not help their fellow man, no matter what! They are just out for themselves. But, I would include 3rd party networking, as well. I have received some excellent candidates this way.

Obviously, this is a longer process than it looks and it can be the most fun, or aggravating part, as well. Do not get discouraged. If you cannot get any names when you call, try calling at different times of the day. Sometimes, the best way to get names is to call very early, or at lunchtime when someone else is filling in for the normal receptionist. As I stated at the beginning of this chapter, research and sourcing is an art, and it is also the most important part of the search assignment, and now you can see why. If you are off the mark in any part of this step it will throw the whole thing off, which becomes very aggravating.

Nobody said recruiting is easy. Directly recruiting gainfully employed candidates is very involved and a lot of work, but if you do your research and sourcing well, it will become a lot easier. Believe me, when you master this step and start recruiting and placing excellent candidates, "heads and shoulders" above anything your client is used to seeing, that's when it will all pay off.

Now that you have the names of the individuals you need within the targeted companies, let's move on to the recruiting process.

Chapter 11

THE RECRUIT

As stated in a previous chapter, the candidates in our business are the product. The clients hire us to find excellent candidates for their positions. At what point does a recruit become a candidate? Well, that's a good question and one that we will get into in this chapter.

The recruiting part of the search assignment is very time consuming and can also get very aggravating. Sometimes it requires a lot of nights and weekends, because the candidates cannot talk during the day. The way you have to think about recruiting is, it is basically the flip side of the search assignment. Everything you asked the client during the search assignment is what you are going to ask the recruit during the recruiting process.

As with the pre-search and search assignment, you are looking for potential problems with the recruit. You are looking for anything that may cause a red flag. As in, a potential counter-offer candidate, someone just looking for more money, job jumpers, etc.

There are a number of issues to consider in general, and there could be many more specific to your industry. We will cover the more basic general issues that you will come across, regardless of your industry. I urge you to come up with your own list of issues and concerns that will be specific to your industry. As with the search assignment, you should have some type of recruiting questionnaire in front of you when you are speaking to a recruit. Not only some of these questions, but also some questions that are specific to your industry.

Remember when we were putting together a job description and speaking to a potential client during the search assignment? Well, it's the same thing when recruiting a potential candidate. You are basically putting together a resume, with a lot more detailed information that you need to know when dealing with candidates. The same thing applies here as it did with potential clients, don't let a potential candidate try and get you off the phone with "I'll send you my resume" or "It's all on my resume" again, we want to speak to potential candidates in detail. We need to know a lot more about them than what is on their resume.

Hint: Never recruit from your clients! If you are doing this, I highly recommend you stop. Nothing will taint your reputation faster than recruiting from your clients.

Once again, as with the search assignment, if you have a way to approach potential candidates and it is working for you, continue to do what works for you. If, on the other hand, you do not know how to approach a gainfully employed recruit at their place of business, here is an opening statement we have learned from various sources throughout the years, and it works. There are several different versions of this that works, you just have to find out what works best for you and your industry.

First of all, you should put together some type of recruiting script together so you do not stumble over your words. Some people do not like working with "scripts" so if you are one of those people, let's call them "notes".

When you call a recruit, you should approach them in a very direct way with your opening statement and explain who you are and why you are calling. For example, "My name is Mike Palumbo and I am in the executive recruiting business". Next you want to tell them the reason for your call. For example, "We are currently recruiting for one of our best clients for a vice president and your name was forward to us as someone well qualified" At this point you want to know if the candidate can speak privately. For example, "Can you talk privately?" If they cannot talk, see if they can move to another phone, or if you can get a phone number to call them later. If they say, yes I can talk, you should move into the fact that your conversation is strictly confidential. For example, "I want to assure you that this conversation is strictly confidential and there are absolutely no costs or obligations on your part, everything will be paid by our client." And, lastly you want to give them information about your client and what you are looking for. For example, "let me give you a little bit of information about our client, our client is…" and then you give a very generic description of your client and what you are looking for without disclosing your client's identity.

Hint: It is very important that you speak slowly and do not ramble during your opening statement with a recruit. You may only have one shot at getting this recruit and turning them into a candidate.

So, if we put it all together your opening statement to any potential candidate it will sound something like this:

"My name is Mike Palumbo and I am in the executive recruiting business. We are currently recruiting for one of our best clients for a vice president and your name was forward to us as someone well qualified. Can you talk privately? (Wait for an answer, if yes) I want to assure you that this conversation is strictly confidential and there are absolutely no costs or obligations on your part, everything will be paid by our client. Let me give you a little bit of information about our client our client is…"

Now that you have the recruit's attention, they are either going to tell you they are "happy" right now and not interested, or they are interested in hearing what you have to offer. If you happened to contact a recruit that is interested in hearing what you have to offer, that is great! Just continue with your recruiting questionnaire and ask them if they have a current resume and have them send it to you. If, on the other hand, they say they are currently "happy" where they are, you have your work cut out for you. A lot of times these types of recruits are uncomfortable speaking to you at work, or they are busy and cannot really speak to you at the moment. If you sense this might be the case, you can give them your phone number and ask them to call you when they are free to speak. You can also ask if they have a different phone number and time they would like you to contact them. Usually, if this recruit has any interest, even if it is very mild interest, they will give you a different phone number and request you contact them later, or they may request a phone number where they can contact you later. You may find some candidates will want to give you a private e-mail address to contact them, as well.

Hint: *It is very important that you respect the potential candidates time and confidentiality. Remember, you are calling them at their place of business, unannounced. If you do not respect their time and start rambling, they might not speak to you again.*

Remember, we want gainfully employed candidates that are not looking, right? That is really what are clients are looking for "top performers" "top talent" so you need to do everything you can to get this recruit to visit with you and maybe possibly turn into a candidate.

If a recruit tells you they are "happy" in their current position and they are not interested in speaking to you later. What do you do? Well, there are some things that can turn a recruit and get them interested, but you really do not want to twist anyone's arm to get them to become a candidate.

If a recruit says something like this "I am perfectly happy here" you can respond by saying something like this "that is precisely why I am calling you, the best time to explore an opportunity is when you are gainfully employed and <u>not</u> on the job market. Do you know why? Because you are dealing through strength when you are <u>not</u> looking. You will tend to evaluate a position in greater detail than if you were out looking. The worst time to explore an opportunity is when you are out of work, or soon to be out of work, that is when we tend to compromise and settle for less than what we can have".

If you absolutely cannot turn this recruit, you will need to roll into "whom do you know we can speak to?" and then I like to add "we will keep your name completely confidential" Lastly, if this particular recruit is still not interested, or willing to give you names, you need to give them your phone number and say "if we can ever be any help to you or your company, let me know" and then move on.

Those are just some of the ways you can get a recruit to speak to you, even if they are "happy" in their current position. Obviously, if you have developed ways throughout your career and it works for you, continue doing what works.

Now let's focus on the areas to dig into when speaking to a recruit that are typically <u>not</u> on a resume. These are questions you should ask along with any resume provided by the recruit. You should put together some type of recruit questionnaire to have in front of you when speaking to a potential candidate. Not only some of these questions, but also some questions that are specific to your industry.

If this potential candidate does not have an updated resume to send you, you will have to ask enough questions to put together biographical information to determine if this candidate is qualified for your client's position. For example, you will need to ask about their current title, years they have been in that title with that company, current duties and responsibilities, education, and where they were employed before and what titles they held there.

This is where your earlier research and sourcing will pay off. If you did your research and sourcing right, this recruit should be very close, if not exactly what you are searching for but, whether this recruit seems to match perfectly, or not, they should at least be with a targeted company, or with a company your client competes with. So, how far off are you going to be?

Now that you have an interested recruit and are asking a lot of questions regarding their background and experience. Let's cover the areas you really need to dig into on the recruit questionnaire that are <u>not</u> on resumes.

The areas of the recruit questionnaire you should really dig into are, **compensation**, **relocation**, and the **hopes, dreams and aspiration**s of the recruit. Under these specific areas you should focus on are a list of typical recruit questions to ask. Again, you might want to tailor some of these questions to your specific industry.

<u>RECRUIT QUESTIONS</u>

COMPENSATION

What is your current base salary? Obviously, this is where you will get a little resistance from your recruit. That is normal. You have to let them know this is very important for you to know because you do not want to waste their time, if in fact they are over the salary range for this position.

<u>Hint:</u> *If a recruit is very reluctant to give you their base salary, most likely it is low and they are somewhat embarrassed.*

Did you get a bonus last year? How much? If they didn't get a bonus last year, you need to know if they got one the year before, and how much that one was. If they did get a bonus last year, you need to know how much that one was, and what they are expecting this year. And lastly, you need to know how those bonuses are paid and what month(s) they are paid. It is very important to know these things, especially when it comes to start dates. What if your client wants this candidate to start on January 1st, but this candidate has a bonus they will not receive until March? If you are unaware of this issue, it could be a problem if this candidate receives an offer. You need to know these answers now, so you can relay them to your client and discuss your options. Most likely, if the candidate is receiving a very large bonus, they will want to wait to receive it.

Do you receive a car allowance, or company vehicle? You need to know if they receive a car allowance, or company vehicle and what the details are. If they get a car allowance, what does that allowance cover? Gas? Tolls? Parking? If they get a company vehicle, how does that work? What type of vehicle? Does their company pick-up anything else? Gas? Tolls? Parking? How often do they get a new vehicle? This information will save you time down the road, as well. Once you have all of the details you can compare them to your clients. If there is a potential problem you can deal with it up-front, rather than after this candidate gets an offer and you find out there is a problem.

Do you receive any other benefits? Obviously, they will have some type of medical plan, dental plan, prescription, optical, 401k, profit sharing etc. In some positions you may see, club memberships, private planes and additional executive type fringe benefits. The key here is you need to get all of the details on everything they have and compare it to your client's benefit package. If your client's benefit package doesn't match up to the recruits, you may have some serious problems with this recruit.

RELOCATION

Are you open to relocation? If the position requires your recruit to relocate, you need to know if they are open to relocation up-front. Discuss the area with the recruit, if they are not sure, have them discuss it with their spouse and get back to you. Obviously, you want to avoid relocations whenever possible, but sometimes you have no choice and you have to relocate someone to a particular area. You want to encourage them to discuss this in great detail with their family and do their due diligence, before you move forward with this recruit. Save yourself the aggravation and have them discuss this with their families first, before you speak to your client. If you jump the gun and move forward and your client gets all excited, only to find out later that this recruit will not relocate, you are going to be embarrassed.

Hint: Do not assume you know the answers to any questions when dealing with recruits. We are all different, so ask the questions.

HOPES, DREAMS AND ASPIRATIONS:

What are your career goals? Sometimes you have to prime the pump here and ask "in the next 5 years" to get them to open up. You really need to discuss what kind of career goals the recruit has, if any. This is going to be a big one. You will be surprised at the answers you receive when you ask this question, but regardless of the answers you need to know what kind of career goals they have. It will also give you insights to them and where they think their career should be headed. Once you have a clear understanding of their career goals, this next question is the most important part of this first question.

Are your career goals attainable at your present company? You have to listen closely to the answers you get when you ask this question. If the recruit does not feel that their career goals are attainable at their present company, what does that mean? Well, it means they will have to leave this company to reach their career goals. Now, you have to match their career goals to what your client is looking for and what the potential is at your client. Hopefully, they can reach their goals with your client quicker than their present employer. Remember the chapter about Win, Win, Win! This is what I was talking about. If a person's goals are not being met at their current company they will start to stagnate and be unproductive. That's not good for their career or their present employer. If your client can provide this potential candidate the career goals they are looking for, this is a winning situation for them and your client.

Hint: _If a recruit's goals are not in-line with your client's, do not move forward. Tell the recruit that their goals cannot be met with your client. They will thank you for being honest about the opportunity._

What would be important to you in a new position? When you ask this question, this is where you are going to get real honest answers from your recruit. You will hear things like, "I want to work for a bigger company" or "publicly traded company" or "smaller company" or "I would need a strong stable company with room to grow" or "the company would have to have a good reputation" whatever the answers you get, and you may get industry specific answers here and I couldn't possibly cover all of the possible answers, this is going to be their wish list. Once again, compare this list to your client's opportunity and see if it is a good fit.

Do you have any career concerns? Sometimes you have to prime the pump here, as well, with "with your position, or future?" This is where your recruit is going to give you an honest answer about the concerns they have at their present company. You need to make a list of these concerns because, if this recruit turns into a candidate, these concerns will help you close this search later. As with the other questions, see how they match up with your client's opportunity.

Hint: Most people suffer a quiet desperation with their careers and do nothing about it. They will suffer through life and never make any attempts to change it, until they receive a call form someone like you.

As you can notice by these recruit questions, most of them are rarely answered in a resume. If you are not asking these questions now, include them from now on, it will definitely help you get a better handle on what your recruit wants, and most importantly, if you can help them!

If you cannot help any recruit with their careers, based on the recruit questionnaire, do not present them to your client and set-up interviews. It just wastes everyone times. Be honest and tell them this opportunity you called them about will not help them reach their career goals and address their career concerns.

Hint: Do not wait for a recruit to send you their resume, especially if they have worked at one company a long time. Put together a "bio" based on your questions and present them to your client. It will speed up the process.

So, what makes a recruit a candidate? A recruit becomes a candidate when all of the information, hopes, dreams and aspirations you receive from your recruit falls in-line with your client's. It has to be the right company, position, duties and responsibilities, location, philosophies and compensation for the recruit to become a candidate. Once everything is in-line, and this recruit fits what your client is looking for, the recruit becomes a candidate.

Now you have to call your client and set-up an interview.

Chapter 12

SCHEDULING INTERVIEWS

Now that you have finished all of the research, source and recruiting for your client, it is time to set-up an interview. Do not call your client and set-up an interview without giving them all of your research and information you have gathered, at this point in the search. You have put a lot of work into this search assignment, so let the client know what you have done. If you have been in fifteen to twenty-five companies, give them the names of the companies. If you had any problems with the search assignment, let them know the problems you have been having. If you heard good things about your client in the marketplace, let them know. If you recruited fourteen people to find their first qualified candidate, let them know. Making your client aware of your efforts, and what you heard in the marketplace, just cements your relationship with them and ensures them you are on their team!

Whatever you do, do not email the first qualified candidate's resume to your client without going into the details of the search assignment. If you do, you are missing out on a valuable time to speak to your client about the search, but also about the candidate.

When you email a resume over to your client, it doesn't have the same effect. It doesn't show the work you have done. And, since most companies do not understand what is involved in the recruiting process, it gives you another opportunity to go into detail about your services and what you provide.

Hint: Never let your client think you are a "body shop" by emailing candidates to them without discussing the candidate's background. The only respect you will receive from this client is, "do you have anyone else?"

<u>Here is an example of how to present your first qualified candidate to your client:</u>

"Hello John, the reason for my call is, we have your first qualified candidate for your position. Before I get into their background it is important that you understand we have been in fifteen companies and have recruited eighteen individuals within those companies to identify your first qualified candidate."

"Let me tell you about your first qualified candidate…"

At this point, you want to go into detail on the candidate's background, education, salary, where they live, etc. The last think I say to my client is "what's your schedule look like to meet?" Now, once again, if your research, sourcing and recruiting have been on target, you should have an excellent local candidate for your client. And, the candidate's goals, hopes, dreams and aspirations should match your client's opportunity. You are setting yourself up for a Win, Win, Win!

One thing you cannot guarantee in this business is personality and chemistry. You can guarantee you will find a qualified candidate, but you have no idea if there will be any chemistry between the client and candidate. That is one reason I like to stay local. When you stay local, the candidate and client will have a lot of commonality between them.

They live in the same city so chances are they root for the same professional teams, maybe they went to the same college, same church, who knows?

You will always have a 25% chance of filling every search assignment you take. Look at this example:

25% of the time the client likes the candidate, but the candidate does not like the client.

25% of the time the candidate does like the client, but the client does not like the candidate.

25% of the time the client and the candidate do not like each other.

25% of the time the client and the candidate LIKE each other!

When you factor in a local candidate with local ties to the community that 25% goes up significantly.

You should continue to present candidates this way, until you have an offer. After presenting your first candidate you do not have to go into detail about the companies again, but you defiantly want to present the candidates the same way you did the first time. Again, do not email candidates to clients without contacting them first. That is how the other recruiter's do business; you need to separate yourself from all of those other recruiters.

So what if you get some resistance from your client? Maybe they do not want to meet with your excellent local candidate? Do not get discouraged. If you get some resistance, and I do not care what kind of resistance, you need to say something like this "I am not telling you to hire this person, I am just suggesting you should meet" "if, after you meet with them, they do not meet the criteria of the search, then we can adjust our efforts and head down a new path" This should get them to agree and meet with your candidate. If it turns out to be impossible to get them to meet with your candidate, your search assignment, research, sourcing and recruiting are very badly off. You need to review the search assignment and compare it to your candidate and see if they match up. If they do not, you need to start over and get a new candidate.

Once your client wants to meet with your candidate it is time to get available times to meet for the client and the candidate. The first thing you should tell your client is to look at all available times and days, and to remember the candidate is working so you need to look at nights and weekends.

If you are dealing with a local candidate, try to avoid a phone interview at all costs. Gainfully employed candidates will not come across very well on a phone interview, especially if they are mildly motivated in the first place. You have spent all this work trying to locate an excellent candidate for your client, if you set-up a phone interview and your candidate doesn't sound interested in speaking to your client, or interested in the position, you may have wasted all of your efforts. Always push for an in-house interview with local candidates.

Once you have the days and times you need to get back to your candidate and see which days will work for them. You should always try for the first available time to meet. If the client gives you this week and next week, when you are speaking to your candidate ask them about this week. Forget next week for now. Only use the dates you have for next week if you need them. Once you have your available days you need to confirm in writing to both parties the exact day, time and meeting place. And, as we discussed earlier, on your memo confirming the meetings put contact phone numbers for the client and the candidate, especially if they are scheduled to meet after hours, on the weekends, or somewhere other than your client's office.

Now that you have this first candidate scheduled you can move forward with the second candidate. Never schedule more than one candidate at a time. Only schedule the second candidate when you have the first candidate confirmed. Never present more than one candidate at a time, especially with new clients. What can happen is, they will want to see one of the candidates but not the other one. If you have the first candidate already confirmed, then move to the second, most likely your client will not want to cancel the first. Then you will have both candidates set-up and confirmed. If you give your client a lot of candidates at once they will pick and choose which one they want to meet. The problem with that is, they might pick the wrong candidate. You want them to meet all of your candidates. The best way to achieve this goal is to present one candidate at a time and set-up meetings one at a time.

The reality is, we do not know which candidate is going to get the position, nor do we really care. We just want to find the best possible candidate for the position. If you have been in this business long enough you will understand that sometimes we think that this one candidate is going to get the position, only to find out the client moved forward with someone else. Knowing this fact, you want all of your candidates to meet with your client.

Hint: There is no such thing as a "perfect candidate". The "perfect candidate" is the one that gets an offer and takes the position!

With all parties scheduled and confirmed to meet, now it is time to discuss coaching. Do you coach candidates, or clients? Should you? My answer is absolutely yes! I have had situations that came up during a meeting and if I didn't coach the candidate they would have passed on them for the position. Obviously, you have to coach the candidate and the client before the meeting.

All of these chapters are connected. If you have a search assignment with additional questions not on a job description, you have valuable information to pass along to a candidate. If you have a recruit questionnaire with additional questions not on a resume, you have valuable information to pass along to the client. See how the search assignment and the recruit questionnaire are really just a reverse of one another?

Now, you are armed with valuable information you can share with both parties and you would be doing yourself a disservice if you didn't use that information. Your goal, and this coaching step plays a big part in this, is to be viewed as a consultant to your clients and a career consultant to your candidates. It really separates you from your competition. So, using the search assignment for things the clients is looking for, and using the recruit questionnaire for the things your candidate is looking for is an excellent idea, and the reason why you asked those questions in the first place. Make sure you have these things in front of you when you are coaching your client and candidate.

COACHING THE CLIENT:

Basically for the client, you want to pass along any information that may be helpful in their meeting. So, while you are looking at the candidate recruit questionnaire you can come up with a lot of things this candidate is looking for in a new position with a new company. For example, if this candidate is looking for a position where they can move up into an officers position, and your client has this potential, you want to make sure your client passes this along in their meeting. Any other issues or concerns your candidate relayed to you in their recruit questionnaire, that your client has to offer, make sure your client covers these in the meeting. Most importantly, make sure to remind your client that this candidate is a recruited candidate and should be handed that way. This candidate cannot be treated like someone out of a job, or soon to be. Reiterate that this candidate may act a little differently than someone approaching them and everything should be handled confidentially.

COACHING A CANDIDATE:

Basically for the candidate, you want to make sure they ask a lot of questions about the duties and responsibilities, philosophies, potential, location and any other issues the client mentioned in their search assignment. For example, if the client is looking for a chief information officer, but they would like this person to be "hands-on" and very technical, you need to pass this along to the candidate, so they can stress to the client that they are "hands-on" and very technical. You do not want the candidate to stress these things if they are not true! Only coach the candidate to emphasize the things that are true. You do not want the candidate to lie about their abilities, or pretend they can do something they cannot. Additionally with the candidate you want to make sure they do not discuss money on a first meeting. You want the candidate to evaluate the company, position, location, type of work, philosophies of the company and potential for their career, first.

Hopefully you are getting the general idea here, you just want to make sure nothing falls between the cracks. The client needs to know what to cover when they meet with any candidate and the candidate needs to know what to discuss when they meet with the client. You are being very helpful to both parties and they will thank you.

Now that you have all the parties scheduled, confirmed in writing, and coached, now what? Let the meetings take place and then do your follow-ups. At this point you may have to do these steps several times, with several candidates and meetings. When you are doing your follow-ups with the client you are refining your search each time. With new clients this is very important because you have never worked together and they have never hired from you. With an existing client you can predict what they will do, how many candidates they need to see, when they will make an offer, etc.

When you are doing your follow-ups with the candidate you are basically seeing if they are interested in proceeding, what their interest level is, and if they are willing to go on another meeting. A lot of times, that is all you should be looking for from candidates. You want to move them to the next step.

The most important question when conducting follow-ups with the candidate, or the client, is really to see if there is any interest in meeting again. Basically on a first meeting, that's it. On a second meeting, or third meeting it might be a little more detailed to see if you are getting closer to an offer. Until you hear the word "offer" you should keep on recruiting and setting up interviews with your client. Other questions you might ask when you are following up with a client or a candidate are; how did it go? How long did you meet? Typically, the candidate or client will start giving you feedback at this point. Usually, the client will be the first to show if there is interest. You may hear something from the client like "when can we get this person back for a second interview?" or "we really liked her" "she really fits into our organization" The candidate may be a little slower to show their hand, because they are gainfully employed and <u>not</u> looking, just exploring. Sometimes they can play it very close to the vest, so to speak. You may hear the candidate say something like "it went okay" "they seems like good people" "I think they are trying to do the right things" you get the picture.

If a client passes on a candidate right away, you need to tell the candidate right away, so they can get on with their life. If a candidate passes on a client and their opportunity right away, you need to tell the client, so you can move on to other candidates.

Regarding that 25% chance of filling all of your positions, as we discussed earlier. As you can see there is a tremendous amount of work to get to the point when you have a candidate that is interested in a position and a client that says those magic words "We want to make an offer" finally, you say to yourself. Well, not really, this is just the start of another beginning. The offer.

Chapter 13

THE OFFER

Finally, you hear your client say they want to make an offer to one of your candidates. Well, let's hope they pick the candidate that will accept the offer!

When you are first starting out in this business it seems that when you finally have a candidate that wants to proceed and accept an offer, the client doesn't want to make <u>that</u> candidate an offer. And, when you have a client that finally says the words "offer" the candidate they want to make an offer too, isn't interested. Very frustrating.

The one way you can avoid this frustrating process is to work a heavier caseload. New recruiters are always working too light. They will hang on every search assignment like it's do, or die. And, usually, it is. The only way to get better in this business is to build-up your caseload.

Since the offer is our "goal line", to use a sports analogy, you need to act like you have been there before. And the only way you can act like you have been there before is to work a heavier caseload and have these situations come up more often. Plus, getting across the "goal line" is more fun!

It is very rewarding to help your client fill a key position, and it is very rewarding to help leverage a candidate's career. If it all comes together you will hear "thank you" from the candidate and the client. That is what this business is all about. If you stay focused on the fact that you have a dual obligation, one to the client, but one also to the candidate, and if you have followed all of the steps to this point and kept consulting with the candidates about their careers, and clients about how they can attract "top talent" to their firm. It is a very rewarding process.

Hint: Most deals fall through, for whatever reason, so you need to have as many searches in the offer stage as you can. If you only have one search a month moving into the offer stage, you will not be very successful in this business.

Now that you have reached the offer stage, it is very important that your client puts together a good offer for your candidate. Nothing can be more frustrating then getting to this stage and the client making a bad, or low offer. This is where your search assignment questionnaire comes in. I told you everything is tied together, right? Remember during the search assignment when you were asking your client about compensation? Make sure you have all of the initial search assignment information in front of you when you are speaking to your client about an offer. Good, or bad.

The first thing you should ask your client when they say they would like to make your candidate an offer is "what type of offer did you have in mind?" Let your client go into the details of the offer, the base salary, car or car allowance, bonuses, 401k, medical plan, dental, optical, relocation (if needed) and any additional benefits. Make sure you write all of the details down when your client gives them to you.

Now, have the recruit questionnaire in front of you and take a look at the candidate's answers on the questionnaire and compare them to what your client is offering.

Is this offer in-line? Is it a good offer? Is it a bad, unacceptable offer?

If the offer is good, confirm this fact with your client "this is an excellent offer" then proceed to have your client put it in writing and present it to your candidate. I always like to put offers in writing, so to avoid confusion down the road. The last thing you want is a candidate that says he was promised something and the client didn't deliver, so putting the offer in writing will avoid this. Your client, candidate, and your firm will all have a record of the offer, so if anything comes up later, you will all have a record of the offer. You should never leave it to your memory. If something comes up a year or two later you will not remember every single detail of this offer.

In my view, a good offer for a local candidate should be at least a 20% increase on the candidate's total compensation. An acceptable offer is anything in the 15% to 20% range, but it really depends on the situation with the candidate and their motivations. If a candidate is very motivated they may accept an offer a lot less than 15%, but this would have to be a case-by-case basis.

I had a situation a few years ago when a gainfully employed recruited candidate, with twenty years with one employer, took a cut in pay and relocated. This particular candidate was in a company where he could not advance without a college degree. He was seeing people advance above him through the years and he finally had enough. Our client wasn't so concerned about his college education they wanted someone who could do the job. As of today, this candidate is the vice president of operations for a very good company, and that opportunity was never attainable with his past employer. The funny thing is, he probably would still be with his old employer if we didn't recruit him for our client. This guy was not looking, just suffering through life in a constant miserable state with a dead end job. This was a Win, Win, Win! But certainly not the norm, so you have to evaluate every offer against your particular situation.

Never let the client offer anything less than a 20% increase on total compensation when dealing with relocation. When you have to deal with relocation, you are really going to have to dig into the relocation package.

Once again, refer to your search assignment questionnaire when speaking to your client about their relocation package. You will always want some type of interim living expenses for a determined amount of time, house-hunting trips for the family, all relocation expenses paid when moving, and any other benefits your client may provide. Basically, this should not cost your candidate anything to move to your client's location. They don't need to make money on this, but certainly it should not cost them anything.

Every situation regarding offers is so different. Once again, you could write a whole book on how to make offers. It is impossible for me to cover every situation you might run into when dealing in the offer stage. The bottom line is, you want the offers to be good. Will it guarantee that the candidates will accept a position with your clients? No, but it will make your life a lot easier and you will make more placements if your client's are making good offers, believe me.

If the offer is bad, you need to address this with your client as soon as possible. Do not let bad offers be extended! Bad offers extended to gainfully employed recruited candidates are the kiss of death. If you let a bad offer be extended and the candidate turns it down it will be very difficult, if not impossible, to get this candidate interested again. We all have stories of candidates that turn down positions and we get them to change their mind based on new information, or something that wasn't covered initially, but once you start down the trail of a turn down the chances are very slim to turn it around.

A very small percentage of candidates, once they have turned down a position, are ever going to change their mind. There are several reasons why. Some candidates will get gun shy, and they won't trust your client again. Some candidates will get offended, and a little mad they went through the process only to be given a low-ball offer.

Some of our clients are trying to save money. They will make a bad offer to "see what the candidates says" or "let's see if we can get him for this amount first, and then if he wants more money we'll see what he comes back with" No, no, no. Always advise your clients to give it their best shot up-front, because with gainfully employed candidates not looking, they may only get one chance.

Whatever the reasons for the bad offer, you need to go back to your search assignment and start addressing the issues of the offer with your client one-by-one.

Remember when we were discussing the search assignment I said you must be looking for future problems with the search, I was speaking about all aspects of the position, including compensation. So, maybe the bad part of the offer is the relocation package, or the car allowance, or the benefit package, or something else. The key here is, you have exactly what the client told you before you started recruiting for this position, right in the search assignment questionnaire. If their offer is different then what your client told you they would do in the search assignment questionnaire, you need to be very firm and address this with them. If you cannot get them to change the offer for your candidate, pass on this company and their supposed "opportunity". You should not recruit for this company again until you have an understanding that they will pay market value, or above, for any of your candidates.

Hint: *It is very important that your client handles your gainfully employed recruited candidates differently than out of work, or soon to be out of work candidates that have approached them. Especially when extending offers.*

I know this can be harsh, but this is a difficult business and a lot of work goes into the research, source and recruiting to fill these positions, even with good offers! Do not frustrate yourself with bad companies that make bad offers.

Always keep doing your business development and looking for good companies that make good offers. A lot of the problems you deal with are self-inflicted, due to the fact that you need the business and are working too light. Because of this, you start recruiting for companies you shouldn't, and you start dealing with candidates you shouldn't, and pretty soon you are "wishing" and "hoping" that a deal comes together.

When most of your placements go sour, you can always go back and look at the pre-search, or search assignment, and there lies the problem. Because you wanted to recruit for this company, and the level of the position they gave you, you overlooked some serious flaws in the search.

There is so much involved with this business, sometimes I wonder how these placements come together at all. The client has to do the right things, as well as be an excellent company. The candidate has to be "top talent" and do the right things during the interviews. Your firm has to consult both parties, every step of the way, and keep things moving along towards an offer. The offer has to be a good offer and acceptable to the candidate, and then you have a placement!

All of the previous steps lead to this step, the offer. If you performed any of the other steps poorly chances are your placement will fall apart. If you rushed through the pre-search and really didn't ask a lot of questions. If you rushed through the search assignment, or candidate questionnaire, and didn't question the answers you received. If you rushed through your research and sourcing to get the names of the recruits you needed. Everything you did will lead you to this final step of the offer or our "goal line" or "pot of gold".

Now that you have an offer, acceptance and start date, it's time to schedule your follow-ups. I recommend you follow-up with the candidate and client a few weeks after the start date to make sure the transition is going smoothly. You want to pass along any feedback to the client and candidate when you do these follow-ups. If there are any problems you will want to know sooner, rather than later, so you can deal with those. Hopefully there are no issues or problems.

Now for the exciting part, depending on how you bill your services, you finally get to invoice your client for all of your hard work!

Chapter 14

BILLING YOUR SERVICES

As you know, we have covered a lot of information regarding your recruiting services, but we haven't touch once on the money, or how to bill your services. That has been by design. The key to this business is to keep your focus on consulting your clients and candidates. Do not think about the money and let it taint your judgment. In the end, it is better to do the right thing for your client and any candidates you may be helping with their careers. The money will come to those recruiters that keep their focus on the important things. We are ultimately in the life changing business. We change people's life for the better and we help companies grow. Do not forget this.

There are so many ways to bill your services, and if what you are doing is working for you, keep doing what you are doing. The reason I put this chapter in this book is because I wanted to share some ideas on a few different ways you may not have thought of when billing your services. If you are doing some of these now, that is great! If not, you may want to try some of these and see if they work for you.

One thing I should point out, all of these examples are based on the total compensation of the candidates we place with our clients. How do we know what the total compensation will be? We do not know what that will be, so it is standard in our industry to estimate what that will be. So when I am discussing the estimated total compensation of a candidate that is an estimate of what the base salary, year-end bonuses, and any sign-on bonuses your candidate can expect to receive. The following examples are just different ways you can bill your services. The more ways you can create revenue to your firm, the better. I use all of these in one form, or another.

1) Traditional retainer
2) Retainer, plus
3) Annual retainer
4) Hourly rate
5) Contingency

Adjust the fees in these examples to fit your firm and your salary ranges and search levels. Now, let's go into detail on each one of these.

TRADITIONAL RETAINER OR 1/3, 1/3, 1/3:

This is a great way to bill your services, if you can get it. A lot of true Executive Search Firms work this way, especially for very senior level executive positions, but in recent times even some of these firms have gone away from this type of billing.

There are many different variations of the traditional retainer, but basically it works like this:

33%, or 1/3, of the estimated total compensation of the position becomes your estimated fee. For example, let's say the estimated total compensation for the position your client wants you to search for is $450,000.

For this example let's use 1/3. You would take 1/3 of that figure, which is $150,000 and then divide this figure by 3, which is $50,000 In this scenario you would bill the client $50,000 three times, plus expenses.

TRADITIONAL RETAINER EXAMPLE:

$50,000 (first 1/3 of the estimated fee) is due when you start the search

$50,000 (second 1/3 of the estimated fee) is due after 30 days

$50,000 (third and final 1/3 of the estimated fee) is due after 60 days whether you fill it, or not.

You would bill the client any additional expenses, up and beyond, the retainer fee, plus you would have to adjust to the actual numbers of the total compensation of the candidate, if you fill the position.

This particular way of billing is not very typical for the thousands of recruiting firms out there. I would not even try this type of billing, unless you are already employed with a firm that bills this way, or you are leaving a firm to start you own firm and you have a client base that is already used to you billing them this way. If you are just starting our in the recruiting business, I would not recommend the traditional retainer.

RETAINER, PLUS:

This is a fantastic way to bill your services and we use this one on a daily basis. If you start billing your services this way, it is an excellent way to ease your way into the more traditional retainer, if you want to go that way. This is a way to get some money up-front, plus expenses, and the balance of the fee at the completion of a search assignment. It also provides a gauge on how serious a company is about filling a position. At the very least you should always start with a "retainer, plus". You can always drop down to a contingency.

The reason why I call this method the "retainer, plus" is because you can bill your client a retainer when you get started on the search, plus expenses, and then the balance of the placement fee when you fill the search. The retainer part, under this method becomes a down payment, and gets deducted from the total fee due, at the completion.

There are many different variations of the "retainer plus", but basically it works like this:

33%, or 1/3, of the estimated total compensation of the position becomes your estimated fee. For this example, let's say the estimated total compensation for the position your client wants you to search for is also $450,000. You would take 1/3 of that figure, which is $150,000 and that number would be your total fee due when you fill the position. In this scenario you would bill your client $150,000 plus expenses when you fill the position, but because you are charging a retainer (down payment) to get started, the final invoice would be adjusted to show the retainer (down payment) they paid to get started.

How much should the retainer (down payment) be? Well some recruiting firms like to take 1/3 of that total fee due as a retainer (down payment), however you can do a flat fee, or a percentage, or 1/3, it is really up to you. What we do is, if the position is a lower, to middle management position we may charge a flat rate of $10,000 as a retainer and for a more senior level position, or executive position we may charge a flat rate of $50,000 or 1/3 of the estimated total fee. But, it really doesn't matter because you will be subtracting it from the final invoice anyway. With the "retainer, plus" method you really have a lot of flexibility.

RETAINER, PLUS EXAMPLES:

If we use a total estimated fee of $150,000 with the "retainer, plus" method you can do several things with this client.

A flat rate:

$10,000 retainer (down payment) to get started on the search and then the balance of $140,000 will be due when you fill the position.

1/3 down:

$50,000 retainer (down payment) to get started on the search and then the balance of $100,000 will be due when you fill the position.

A percentage:

10% down, which is a $15,000 retainer (down payment) to get started on the search and then the balance of $135,000 will be due when you fill the position.

You would also bill the client any additional expenses, up and beyond, the retainer fee, plus you would have to adjust to the actual numbers of the total compensation of the candidate, when you fill the position. If you notice, I use the term "down payment" with the retainer. The reason why is because some companies have an aversion to paying retainers, but amazingly when you discuss a "down payment" they totally understand that and are more open to it. So, if you are having trouble getting retainers, try changing your wording to "down payment". It's simple and it works!

ANNUAL RETAINERS:

This is another fantastic way to bill your clients, and a great way to help on your cash flow. This is not something I would ever present to a new client, only very good existing clients. We have used annual retainers now for several years and they work very well with repeat clients that work very slowly.

We all have them. The clients that take forever to make decisions on candidates, it takes them forever to make offers, and they work very slowly. I am not saying you cannot use this with clients that move at a faster pace it's just a great tool to use on the slower clients.

Some recruiters are reluctant to present annual retainers for fear that they will miss out on money, or lose control of the situation and end up working on very low level positions. I find just the opposite is true.

First of all, it really cements your relationship with the client and you become a real member of the team. They can count on you, rely on you, and look to you for professional guidance on the growth of their company. You need to set the ground rules up-front so you don't end up working on low level positions, or positions that are not conducive to the way you work. You work on the same positions as before, but now you have a client that pays you every month.

Don't get me wrong, sometimes we have had clients on annual retainers want us to do exit interviews, or something along those lines, and we will charge them extra to do that type of work. Even though we don't do that type of work on a regular basis and we certainly do not look for work like this, if we didn't have them on an annual retainer would they have called us? I don't think so. It's another revenue stream for your firm.

There are many different variations of annual retainers, but basically it works like this:

The basic way to set-up annual retainers is to take the estimated placement fee of a search assignment and divide it up annually. What if the estimated placement fee is $150,000? Now you can divide this fee up annually for $12,500 a month for twelve months. Let's take this a step further. What if the estimated placement fee included two positions? One that has a fee of $150,000 and one that has a fee of $150,000 now you can add up these two fees and get a $300,000 estimated placement fee. Now you can divide that fee up annually and come up with $25,000 a month for twelve months. Of course, up and beyond this monthly recurring fee, your client would be responsible for any expenses incurred during the search process.

Once again, I would only present something like this with an existing client that you have had a relationship and history with. Another way to present something like this is to say to your client, "how many searches will you have us work on this year?"

If your client is in a growth mode they may have several, but if you have a history with this client and you know in the past you have averaged two placements a year, you can take an average placement fee of the two positions, add those up and divide it by twelve. For example, if your average placement fee with this client is $50,000 and you typically do two placements a year with them, you can add the two fees and get $100,000 and divide that up annually for $8,333.33 a month. Now for $8,333.33 a month you will work on all of the assignments for this firm and once you fill two positions with them, you would then start billing them for the third position and so on. Of course, after filling the second position with this company you will be back to your regular billing procedure, only this time you also have a recurring billing amount of $8,333.33 a month.

If you get some resistance when presenting your annual retainer, you can always tell your client that the annual retainer can be reviewed every six months, and adjusted accordingly. It could be raised, or lowered, depending on the situation. Annual retainers help out tremendously on cash flow. With annual retainers you really become a member of your clients team. I wouldn't do them with every client you have, but it does give you another way to bill those slow working clients.

ANNUAL RETAINER EXAMPLES:

If your client has a yearly average placement fee of $150,000, with the annual retainer you can do several things with this client.

Annual monthly fee:

Take the $150,000 fee and divided it into twelve months for $12,500 a month and work on all of their search assignments for the year. This would be worked out prior to placing your first candidate, with reviews every six months for any adjustments. If they hire six people in six months and go over that $150,000 estimated fee, you need to adjust your annual retainer up. If, on the other hand, they are not on target with that $150,000 number after six months, you still have the balance of the year to get there. At the end of the year you should review this with your client and see if it needs adjusted.

Annual monthly fee, with placement fee:

Take the $150,000 fee and divide it into twelve months for $12,500 a month and work on all of their assignments for the year. Again, this has to be worked out prior to placing your first candidate, with reviews every six months for any adjustments. With this plan your client is going to pay you $12,500 a month based on your estimated fee of $150,000 and then the client would start paying your regular billing rate after you have reached $150,000. Basically every placement you make with this company, your usual fee would be subtracted from that $150,000. Now you may reach that number in three or six months, or it may take all year. This plan helps the client budget their recruiting fees better and it helps you with your cash flow.

Annual monthly fee, with a bonus:

Take the $150,000 fee and divide it into twelve months for $12,500 a month and work on all of their assignments for the year. Again, this has to be worked out prior to placing your first candidate, with reviews every six months for any adjustments. With this plan your client is going to pay you $12,500 a month and a flat rate bonus after you have reached $150,000 In this case, I would start the flat rate bonus at $10,000 for every placement. Now, if the estimated yearly fee is higher, you can make the flat rate bonus higher, as well. Under this plan your client wouldn't have to worry about you billing them your regular fee which can be another $75,000 or $150,000 for every placement once you have reached that $150,000 number. This is a good deal for your client and it helps them with their budgeting and it helps you with your cash flow.

As you can see, there are several ways to bill your client an annual retainer. You can probably come up with some of your own, as well. It is important that you set the ground rules up-front on annual retainers. It is an excellent way to bill your clients that work very slowly. You will be surprised at the reception you get with annual retainers. In some cases, it is easier to justify and budget for your clients, especially if it is difficult for them to pay the substantial recruiting fees.

HOURLY RATE:

This is another way to bill your services where you have that recurring billing that helps with your cash flow. Setting an hourly rate in our business can be a little tricky. It really depends on what you are trying to achieve. If you are interested getting residual income along with your other ways you bill, this is the way to do it. In most cases, this is a great way to move into an annual retainer. We have had clients start out on an hourly basis and when it got to be to cumbersome with paperwork and keeping track of the hours we spent on each search assignment, they requested us to come up with a monthly fee instead.

So, how do you determine the hourly rate? That's a loaded question and it really depends on you.

There are many different ways to bill on an hourly rate, but basically it works like this:

You can take your annual billings and figure out what you are worth, per hour in a year. If you don't like that number you can calculate an hourly rate that you think will equal to the amount of the placement fee for the position and then bill your client that rate. If you are working on several positions you can add up those placement fees and calculate a rate that way. Either way, it has to be something that your client agrees upon and you feel is fair to your firm.

HOURLY RATE EXAMPLE:

Let's say you, not your firm, bills $600,000 a year. Divide $600,000 by 2,080 hours in a year and you get $288/hour. That's basically what you make an hour. If you feel in your market, or industry, that amount is to high you can calculate a workable hourly rate of $200/hour, if you think that is something that would work better for your client. If you bill a lot more in a year your hourly rate is obviously going to be higher.

This is the best way calculate your hourly rate, because it can be to difficult to get an hourly rate based on a placement fee amount and the usual time it takes you to fill the search, because there isn't a usual time. Under this plan you would bill your client until the position is filled, or stopped by your client. I would also recommend you set up some type of billing schedule with your client, either every two weeks, or once a month.

Obviously, the hourly rate you calculate will be per search assignment. If they want you to work on multiple searches it will be that hourly rate per search. You could feasibly be sending several invoices to this client a month for all of the positions they have you working on per hour. In some cases, you may want to put a limit to the amount you can bill. So, if the estimated placement fee is $150,000 once you reached $150,000 with your hourly billings it would stop.

Our firm has had great success with the hourly rate plan to bill our services. The client is basically paying the same thing, just spread out over the life of the search assignment. And, it helps with your cash flow.

CONTINGENCY:

This is the last and worst way to bill your services. Always present the other ways to bill your service first. You can always fall back on a contingency, why? Because it has absolutely no risk to the client! You have all of the risk when working on contingency. I realize when you are starting out and building up your practice you have to take some contingency work. It will be up to you to build your caseload to the point where you are so busy you cannot possibly take on another search assignment on contingency. At that point, you can start presenting retainers to any future clients and you will start to get retainers. The only way to get retainers is to ask. Always present retainers first before you roll into a contingency, and once you build your caseload up significantly, never work on contingencies again.

There are many different ways to bill under a contingency agreement, but basically it works like this:

You bill the client when they hire one of your candidates. There is absolutely no financial obligation whatsoever to your client until they hire someone. These clients can put you on a wild goose chase so make sure they are serious about filling this search assignment before you start recruiting. Make sure you have everything in writing, and signed by the client before you start recruiting. Make sure you put exactly what the fee amount would be and when it would be due, if they hired one of your candidates.

CONTINGENCY EXAMPLE:

If the total compensation on the offer and the candidate accepts is $450,000 the client would pay you a percentage of that total compensation. If your firm charges a fee for your services of 30% of total compensation, it would look something like this.

$450,000 x 30% = $135,000

$135,000 would be paid to you only if the candidate starts with your client. Obviously, if your percentage is less your fee is going to be less.

You need to be cautious about performing contingency work. There is absolutely no risk to the client. You need to make sure you do a pre-search and search agreement, in detail. If you feel this company is serious about hiring, but they have a policy in their company that says they will not pay retainers to recruiters, then I would move forward but very cautiously. At the very least, this would have to be a very good company with an excellent position.

And finally, our firm bills under most of these plans. We will have some clients under the "retainer, plus" "annual retainers" "hourly rate" and "contingency" plans all at once. It gives us a little variety and flexibility when it comes to our clients, and we always know where our money is coming from. We can budget because we know the amount of money, at the very least, we will be getting in every month.

So, I urge you to try some new ways to bill your service.

CONCLUSION

We are in a very unique business as an executive search, or professional recruiter. We get to see the inside workings of some of the best companies in the world. We get to know these companies inside and out, how they operate, how they function internally and what makes these companies so successful.

We can influence the way they do business, and we teach them how to attract "top talent" to their firm. We play a role that's not often discussed, but we're there. They rely on us. They need us. It's impossible for them to attract the "top performers" they will need to sustain any type of growth.

We provide insights to the industry, market research, and salary survey's. When it comes to finding and securing the best possible talent in their industry, we are their "secret weapon".

In regards to candidates, we help them leverage their careers. We help them achieve their hopes, dreams and aspirations in their careers and life.

<u>We are in the life changing business.</u>

This business has seen some changes in recent years, especially with technology. Web sites that advertise positions and recruits looking for positions. What's next? What does the future hold for our business? Will there be a need for us in the future?

Absolutely! Now more than ever! The web sites are nothing more than glorified newspaper classified sections. The available candidates on these web sites are the same people that are always looking for jobs, we just have a lot more of them now, and now we get them from all around the world!

Technology has been fantastic for our industry in some ways. We no longer have a ton of yellow pages in our office from all over the country. We can get personal information on an individual a lot quicker. Researching and doing our due diligence on potential clients is a lot faster. Most companies now have web sites.

The bottom line is, the technology is great but you still have to visit with a potential client and get a feel for their overall corporate philosophies and how they do things. You still have to research and source a potential candidate, because the individuals we want for our clients are gainfully employed and <u>not</u> looking. These types of candidates are not circulating their resumes in the marketplace; you have to dig these individuals out.

The main reason there is a bright future for us, regardless of technology, is the <u>confidentially</u> of our services. It is crucial to our clients and candidates that everything be handled in the strictest of confidence when performing our research, source and recruiting functions. <u>That's key</u>.

I hope the information in this book will help you achieve your hopes, dreams and aspirations in your career as an executive search, or professional recruiter. Although this can be a very frustrating business, it can also be a very rewarding business.

I hope you obtained a couple of *hints* in this book that will assist you in your day-to-day operations and maybe open your eyes to a couple new ideas.

I want you to be the best executive search or professional recruiting firm in the world! And, I hope in some little way this book helps you get there!

Good luck!

ABOUT THE AUTHOR

Michael J. Palumbo is the founder of The Palumbo Company, an Executive Search and Professional Recruiting firm, headquartered on the Gulf Coast of the United States in Fairhope, Alabama.

For more information regarding recruiting techniques, research and sourcing, training seminars, business development techniques and career consultation call or write:

The Palumbo Company

PO Box 1998

Fairhope, AL 36533

www.thepalumbocompany.com

CPSIA information can be obtained at www.ICGtesting.com
Printed in the USA
BVOW08s0803130815

412999BV00003B/210/P